BASEBALL

365

DAYS

JOSEPH WALLACE

AN OFFICIAL PUBLICATION FROM THE ARCHIVES OF MAJOR LEAGUE BASEBALL

ABRAMS, NEW YORK

I'm writing this introduction in August 2007, just a few days after Tony Gwynn and Cal Ripken, Jr., were inducted into the Baseball Hall of Fame. I have to admit that when I heard they were eligible, my first thought was, "That can't be! They're too young!" But it was true: These two superb players retired in 2001, making them ready to gain deserved first-ballot entry into the Hall this year. The fact that I have such vivid memories of watching them play says as much about how long I've been a baseball fan—forty years and counting—as about these particular athletes.

Most of my previous baseball books have focused on the greatest players of baseball's various "golden ages" of the past, from Ty Cobb to Walter Johnson to Babe Ruth to Joe DiMaggio to Ted Williams to Sandy Koufax. This is the first book I've written that concentrates instead on the superstars from 1970 to the present. It is my own "golden age," because I lived through it and got to watch most of the players when they were in their prime, either live or on television. I grew up idolizing them, marveling at their skills, enthusiasm, and love for a game I love as well—and I'll bet many of you did, too.

So it was a particular treat to be able to include the spectacular photos you'll find as you page through this book: Ozzie Smith making spectacular fielding plays; ever-enthusiastic George Brett unleashing his sweet swing; Jim Palmer, Steve Carlton, Nolan Ryan, Greg Maddux, Randy Johnson, Roger Clemens, and other pitchers at the height of their prowess; brilliant backstops Thurman Munson and Gary Carter; those idolized Bronx Bombers Don Mattingly and Derek Jeter; quiet superstars Paul Molitor, Robin Yount, Willie Stargell, and Willie McCovey; midcareer legends like David Ortiz and Vladimir Guerrero; and dozens of others. Not to mention fans and mascots and umpires, spring training scenes, ballparks both vanished and existing, and all the other things that make baseball so central to our lives.

I chose to include these photographs because I found them exciting, funny, even moving. But what was most wonderful about them for me is the memories they evoked. A photo of Tom Seaver as a New York Met reminded me of a day in April 1970 when my seventh-grade social-studies class went on an (educational?) field trip to Shea Stadium and saw Tom Terrific strike out nineteen San Diego Padres. Photos from the 1975 World Series instantly carried me back to college in Connecticut, surrounded by rabid Boston fans as the Red Sox waged their valiant—but losing—effort against the Big Red Machine. And a shot of Mariano Rivera wearing a New York Police Department cap at the 2001 Series brings back all the memories of 9/11... and the way the magnificent World Series pitting the Yankees against the Arizona Diamondbacks allowed us to look forward again.

I hope that these images are as meaningful to you.

People always ask me where I find the photos in my books. That was one of the biggest treats of working on this project: I was given access to Major League Baseball's vast and rich archives and told to take my time to find the images I liked the best. It was the most enjoyable treasure hunt you could imagine... day after day surrounded by Roberto Clemente, Kirby Puckett, Johnny Bench, Mike Schmidt, and so many others.

As you turn the pages, you'll see that I also searched for the stories behind the photos: the perfect quote, telling detail, amusing insight. In many cases, such as World Series games, that was a relatively easy task. But for other images—including some of my favorites—I could see that there was a story there, but I didn't know exactly what it was. (What's up with those dancing baseball gloves on page 375 or that mitt Chet Lemon is holding on page 353, anyway?)

Maybe you can help. The true richness of baseball's past relies on the stories fans tell, the facts they reveal. If you know anything I don't mention in the captions, please feel free to drop me a line, and I'll pass your information on to the archivists at MLB. Just contact me through my website, www.josephwallace.com. I'll be glad to hear from you, and you'll be adding to the public knowledge of baseball history.

This book would never have gotten off the ground without the help of the folks at Major League Baseball. In particular, Don Hintze, Vice President of Publishing, who was an early fan of the idea, made the project happen by opening the door to the archives for me. In the photo department, Paul Cunningham (Photo Editor) was ever patient with my questions, fulfilled all my requests without complaint, and pointed me toward his own personal favorite photos—which usually became some of mine as well. And Rich Pilling (Director of Photography) was of incalculable help in two ways: He helped guide me through the archives, and he took many of the finest images reproduced in this book, including many rare shots from the 1970s and 1980s. I must also thank the many other photographers whose fine work is included here; their names are listed in the photo credits.

At Abrams, I'm grateful to Editor-in-Chief Eric Himmel for making this treasure hunt possible and to my incomparable editor, Sharon AvRutick, and designer, E.Y. Lee, for giving this book a vividness and vitality it otherwise would have lacked. Thanks to you all!

Future All-Star?

Every young baseball fan has hopes of someday standing on the diamond of a major-league ballpark. But for some it's a shorter route than for others: Darren Baker, pictured here with his father, San Francisco Giants manager Dusty, was the Giants' batboy when he was just three years old, warming the hearts of fans everywhere and fulfilling a million boyhood dreams.

"Go on Contact, Sweetie."

Oakland A's third-base coach Clete Boyer dispenses advice to Nicola Davis, outfielder Mike's daughter, at a "Bring Your Kids to Work" event in Oakland. From its earliest, humblest days, baseball has captured children's imaginations, instilling a lifelong love of the game. In this multimedia era, with so many other entertainments to distract them, it's more important than ever to help kids maintain their connection with the game.

Young at Heart

Spring-training scene: blue skies, billowing clouds, and a young fan straining to see over the fence to glimpse a field of dreams. "Don't tell me about the world. Not today," wrote Pete Hamill. "It's springtime and they're knocking baseballs around fields where the grass is damp and green in the morning and the kids are trying to hit the curve ball."

An International Game at Last

A hundred years ago baseball magazines were filled with articles about how the game was spreading across the globe, to Europe, the South Pacific, even the Far East. Those articles were, at best, overly optimistic—but baseball came of age internationally by the end of the century. Proof positive: the participation of children from Japan, Canada, Mexico, and even Saudi Arabia in the 1998 Little League World Series, their flags proudly displayed at the contestants' parade.

Young Wizard

With a focus and intensity that would do a major leaguer proud, Toms River, New Jersey, shortstop Todd Frazier helps take his team to the 1998 Little League World Series Championship. Nine years later, Frazier was still at it: As a junior at Rutgers University in 2007, he was unanimously named the Big East Conference Baseball Player of the Year. "When you've played in front of 44,000 people when you're little, that definitely helps you out later," Frazier said upon winning the award.

Standing with the Big Boys

Members of the Japanese 1998 Little League World Series team on a visit to Yankee Stadium. Joining them are Bronx Bombers Scott Brosius (#18), Derek Jeter (#2), and Chuck Knoblauch (#11). Even a decade earlier, these kids' dreams of growing up to play in Yankee Stadium might have seemed like the wildest fantasy, but not today: Japanese players ranging from Ichiro Suzuki through Hideki Matsui and Daisuke Matsuzaka have all established themselves as bona-fide major-league stars since this photo was taken.

For the Kids

In 1989 former major-league player and scout John Young founded Reviving Baseball in Inner Cities (RBI). His goal was to provide inner-city youth with the chance to learn about and enjoy the game, as well as to help instill discipline and a sense of purpose in boys and girls who too often lacked strong role models. Here are some of the players participating in the third annual RBI World Series, held in 1995 in Philadelphia.

Here's the Windup

A pitcher unleashes his best stuff in the 1995 Reviving Baseball in Inner Cities (RBI) World Series in Philadelphia. Starting modestly in South Central Los Angeles, the program has spread to 200 cities across the country and even internationally, attracting 200,000 participants each year. In the words of Roberto Clemente, Jr., founder of the Pittsburgh RBI program, RBI "keeps kids out of trouble and off the streets, while at the same time teaching them to stay in school. They earn self-esteem and self-respect."

That Old College Try

Future major-league star Nomar Garciaparra, a junior at Georgia Tech, takes a big swing during the 1994 College World Series. Unheralded Tech, making its first World Series appearance, came close to capturing a surprising victory before falling to Oklahoma in a Series populated by soon-to-be big leaguers: Garciaparra's future Boston Red Sox teammate Jason Varitek, as well as Mark Kotsay, Mark Bellhorn, Jay Payton, Mark Redmond, and several others.

On the Verge

Though originally signed by the Minnesota Twins out of high school, Bret Boone—like many other modern players—chose to go to college instead. Just two years after graduating from the University of Southern California, where he starred on the Trojans, he was on the field with the Seattle Mariners. Boone's adjustment wasn't as large as for many players: Both his father, Bob, and his grandfather, Ray, were major leaguers themselves.

Voice of Experience

Carlos Delgado, regarded as one of the most thoughtful and outspoken of all ballplayers, shares his wisdom with young players in this shot from 2001. If he was giving them advice on being patient, allowing their talent to develop, and not expecting too much too quickly, Delgado would have been speaking from experience: He hit under .200 during his first two trials with Toronto before finally establishing himself as an up-and-coming All-Star.

Make or Break

Seven years before the previous photo, during his rookie season in 1994, the Toronto Blue Jays' Carlos Delgado must have wondered if his career would ever take off. Though he hit 9 home runs in 130 at-bats, he also struck out 46 times and hit just .215. The next year was even worse: a .165 batting average in 91 at-bats, with just 3 homers. But the Blue Jays were patient, and in 1996 Delgado came through, raising his average to .270, slamming 25 home runs, and driving in 92 runs.

Dawn of Two Superstars

How young they were! University of Texas student Roger Clemens in 1982 and Tom Glavine of the Sumter (South Carolina) Braves in 1985 smile with all the self-confidence of born stars. They had plenty to be happy about: Between Clemens' explosive fastball and Glavine's array of carefully placed pitches, by 2007 the two had combined for 600-plus wins, nearly two dozen trips to the postseason, 9 Cy Young Awards, and certain election to the Hall of Fame.

Blinding

In 2002 at the time of this Futures Game—the annual contest between U.S. and world prospects played every All-Star break—Jose Reyes was merely a nineteen-year-old up-and-comer. He always had extraordinary speed, but a series of leg injuries later threatened to derail his career with the New York Mets. Then, remarkably, the injuries stopped, and Reyes blossomed into one of the most exciting players to arrive in years, becoming a constant threat to steal bases (124 his first two full seasons), hit triples (34 in the same period), and score runs.

The Sure Thing?

In 2000 twenty-year-old Texas Ranger prospect Hank Blalock was laboring in Single-A Savannah. By 2002 he was starting for the big club. In between, he was showcased in the 2001 Futures Game, like so many others a prospect with a world of potential that might or might not be tapped. In this case, the story had a happy ending: In 2003, the fans voted Blalock onto the All-Star Team—and he won the game with a home run against Dodgers closer Eric Gagne.

Maintaining Control

For many young pitchers, the difference between failure and stardom may be just a few inches. From the moment he was signed by the New York Mets in 1995, A. J. Burnett, for example, was a hot prospect with an unlimited ceiling—if he could only master his control. Traded to the Florida Marlins in 1998, Burnett continued to show flashes of brilliance, including throwing a no-hitter in 2001. But he walked an astonishing nine men in the same game, leaving the ultimate assessment of his career an open question.

Playing in Traffic

Next to catching and pitching, there's no position on the diamond riskier than second base. It requires an enormous amount of twisting and sudden movements (hard on the legs), throws from awkward angles (hard on the arms), and, of course, the ever-present danger of collisions at the bag (hard on the whole body). Here, young Orlando Hudson learns a painful lesson from Miguel Cabrera during the 2002 Futures Game.

Getting in Shape for Stardom

In baseball's earlier years, minor-league players often labored in obscurity, hoping against hope for a big break. Today, though, high-profile draft picks, big contracts, new ballparks, and a resurgence in fan support have led to stardom even for players who have never set foot in the bigs. Here, Richmond Brave Chipper Jones makes the day of some enthusiastic fans. (As you can see in the upper left, he already had his own baseball card!)

Young Nomah

On the brink of a brilliant career, Nomar Garciaparra of the Trenton Thunder takes a moment to relax. Major-league teams frequently switch minor-league affiliates, often for financial reasons, and sometimes the result goes against logic. This was true in 1995, when the Red Sox took over the Trenton, New Jersey, affiliate, located squarely in Yankee country. This awkwardness was addressed in 2003: The Sox and Yanks swapped towns, with the Bombers moving their Double-A team into Trenton, and the Sox taking over Portland, Maine, a dyed-in-the-wool part of Red Sox Nation.

Thirty Yards and a Cloud of Dust

Life in the minor leagues is often a grind, not to mention a faceful of dirt. To future Hall of Famer Mike Piazza, though, there were great benefits to the smaller world of the minors as well. "To me, it was the innocence of it," he said, nostalgic for "the camaraderie of the guys, the fact that you're not making a ton of money, that you all have the same dream and you're driven by that dream."

String Drill

Oakland A's catching hopefuls line up in a spring training "string drill." Designed by the great Branch Rickey (the man who signed Jackie Robinson) during his years with the Brooklyn Dodgers, the drill marks off a series of strike zones with strings. This allows several pitchers to work on their control at the same time, with each pitch clearly a ball or a strike. To make the drill more realistic, Rickey would sometimes set up a dummy batter at each home plate.

A Solitary Job

For most pitchers spring training is hard and lonely work. While hitters, arriving in Florida or Arizona in far better shape than players did a generation ago, need only a short period of time to get their timing back and be ready for the season, pitchers must put in hour after hour, gradually regaining their strength and accuracy. The result is a lot of time spent on the mound, with only a catcher, a coach, and a cluster of interested fans in attendance.

Tall Cool One

In the blistering heat of the Arizona midday sun, no one can blame players like Tsuyoshi Shinjo for not assuming the alert "ready position" before each pitch—or for dreaming of a pile of nachos and a bottle of something frosty. Spring-training games are catnip for devoted fans, though, who can sit back and relax, work on their tans, and escape into the shade whenever they feel like it.

The Wisdom of the Ages

An Oakland A's coach dispenses advice to a bunch of fresh-faced hopefuls in Arizona. "You've got a hundred more young kids than you have a place for on your club," Baltimore Orioles' manager Earl Weaver told writer Thomas Boswell. "Every one of 'em has had a goin'-away party. They've been given the shaving kit and the fifty dollars. They kissed everybody and said, 'See you in the majors in two years.'" But in the vast majority of the cases, Weaver lamented, "You see these poor kids who shouldn't even be there in the first place."

On the Ball

Major-league baseballs—which are now made in Costa Rica—have three components: a round cushioned cork core, wool and poly/cotton windings, and a cowhide cover. To pass muster, balls must weigh between 5 and 5.25 ounces and measure between 9 and 9.25 inches in circumference. Amazingly, most baseballs last only six or fewer pitches before being lost or taken out of play. Approximately 900,000 baseballs are used in the major leagues each year in spring training, batting practice, and games.

Dividing Line

Smaller ballparks, a more relaxed attitude, and lots of downtime means that spring-training baseball allows fans closer access to the players than they ever get in the regular season. But not *that* close. To fans, the memento—a signed ball or card—at least reminds them that they live in the same world as Felipe Crespo. For the player, though, too often fans are reduced to gesturing, beseeching masses. True contact can be a challenge.

Saddling Up Again

Great Yankee catcher Thurman Munson (center, helping fellow backstop Mike Heath, with Cliff Johnson in the background) at the start of the 1978 season. "What every fan thinks is thrilling about the game, Thurman was part of, some way—a ninth-inning hit to win the ballgame, a slide in to beat somebody up," recalled Orioles catcher Rick Dempsey after Munson's tragic death in 1979. "Knock them over, knock the ball loose, block the plate, throw somebody out! Thurman was always in the middle of it."

Hanging On

Under the watchful eye of Detroit Tigers' coach Jeff Jones, thirty-nine-year-old Jose Mesa gears up for one more go-round in the spring of 2007. Spring training is filled equally with fresh-faced youngsters hoping to make an impression and grizzled veterans facing the end. Even a talented reliever like Mesa, who at his peak was a closer (he saved forty-plus games four times), has to prove himself all over again. Mesa did make the A.L.-champion Tigers out of spring training, joining his eighth team in nineteen years, and then moved on to the Phillies.

Flippin' Seeds

Oakland A's players make the time pass with a typical spring-training contest. For decades, players who don't chew tobacco but who want to give their jaws a workout have crunched on sunflower seeds. From there, it is only a short step to a contest pitting finger-snapping players against each other to see who could make the seed fly farthest. You never know—maybe flipping seeds could even help prevent Sunflower Seed Finger, a recognized medical condition in which players overstretch their finger ligaments while digging for the next handful of seeds.

Catch of the Day

A young fan and his day's haul—a prize likely to be treasured for a lifetime by a fan with dreams of stepping onto the field himself one day. "When I was a small boy in Kansas, a friend of mine and I went fishing," recalled President Dwight D. Eisenhower. "I told him I wanted to be a real Major League baseball player, a genuine professional like Honus Wagner. My friend said that he'd like to be President of the United States. Neither of us got our wish."

Grunt 'n' Groan

The Cincinnati Reds limber up for a new season. In this age of sophisticated workout technology and year-round training regimens, the sight of professional ballplayers engaging in calisthenics seems almost quaint. In fact, so does almost everything else about baseball in February and March in Arizona and Florida. The great broadcaster Harry Caray had it pegged: "It's the fans that need spring training," he said. "You gotta get 'em interested."

Silhouette Stretches

Players loosen up under a blazing spring sun, hoping to prevent the aches and pains that playing baseball inevitably brings. Professional athletes are healthier today than ever before—as reflected in the great number of careers that last into the players' forties—but despite the relentless focus on fitness and exercise, injuries are still a dangerous, painful possibility at any time.

Dodgertown

Sluggers in the batting cages at Dodgertown, the longtime spring-training complex of the Los Angeles (and previously Brooklyn) Dodgers in Vero Beach, Florida. The Dodgers have been visiting Vero Beach since 1948 and playing in Holman Stadium, the centerpiece of the Dodgertown Complex, since 1953—but spring-training trends have changed radically since then. These days, every other West Coast team journeys to Arizona in the spring, and the call for the Dodgers to move grows louder every year. As of now, though, the team clings to tradition.

Good Enough

A bucketful of stained, scuffed baseballs awaits use in spring-training practice. It's funny that just a few decades ago such balls would have been considered too clean for use in games. The first thing players would do was rub up a new ball with dirt to make it easier to grip and harder for the batter to see. Then many pitchers would add saliva or grease to make it move unpredictably. The dark ball and its extra movement helped allow the pitchers to dominate the game until 1920, when star shortstop Ray Chapman was killed by a pitch he didn't see. After that cleaner balls were put in play and most "freak" pitches—such as spitballs—were outlawed.

Showcase

The Arizona Fall League is a place for young players, ones with uncertain futures, and ones who didn't get enough work during the regular season to show off their skills. Scouts and coaches watch carefully, but no one takes AFL achievements too seriously: It's very common for the season's batting champion to hit over .400—and in 2002 Richard Harvey finished with an astounding .479 batting average. Here is Bubba Trammell, a star with the Peoria Javelinas in the mid-1990s and a useful role player for several teams on the big stage.

One Hard Game to Play

In 1994 the legendary Michael Jordan, still on top of his game, stepped away from pro basketball and decided to try his hand at baseball. It was a stunning decision, and fans worldwide wondered if Jordan could translate his basketball magnificence into success in a very different sport. Sadly, the answer was no: In a single season with the Birmingham Barons (the Chicago White Sox' AA team), Jordan batted just .202—and though he managed to raise that to .252 as a member of the Scottsdale Scorpions in the Arizona Fall League, he soon hung up his spikes and returned to the Chicago Bulls.

Forever on Deck

Everyone shares the same dreams of glory, but the box scores are filled with players who never take the next step to stardom. Billy Ashley, pictured here, had little more than 600 at-bats spread over seven seasons, most spent with the Los Angeles Dodgers. His career numbers—28 home runs, 84 RBI, a .233 batting average—are engraved in the record books alongside those who left a more substantial mark on the game's history... and those who accomplished far less.

The Right Choice

The six-foot-six Dave Winfield had a choice of three sports to pursue out of the University of Minnesota: football, basketball, or baseball. He seems to have selected wisely. After getting a taste of the majors with the San Diego Padres in 1973, when he was just twenty-one, Winfield became a durable star, slamming 465 home runs (including the Opening Day shot in 1978 he's celebrating here with Manager Roger Craig), and accumulating 3,110 hits in a Hall of Fame career.

Starting for the Yankees…Mariano Rivera?!

Only dedicated Yankee fans remember that when he first arrived in the majors in 1995 as a skinny twenty-five-year-old out of Panama City, Panama, Mariano Rivera made ten starts among his nineteen appearances. No one could have predicted from his numbers that season (5.51 ERA, 71 hits, and 30 walks allowed in 67 innings) that just a year later he would be the best setup man in the game, and the year after that the finest closer. Twelve years later those ten starts remain the only times Mo ever set foot on the mound in the first inning.

En Route to Glory

Some great players take years to establish themselves as stars. But not Albert Pujols. Growing up in the baseball-mad Dominican Republic, he arrived in the majors in 2001 as a battle-tested twenty-one-year-old, ready to face the toughest pitching the big leagues could offer. The result: a .329 batting average, 37 home runs, and 130 RBI. "He has a passion for the game, a love for the game," said his hitting coach, former star Mike Easler. "You can see it. You can sense it. He's got natural God-given ability. A natural baseball player. A warrior."

Touching Up Home

The grass is mowed, the dirt is watered, the foul lines are straight, and home plate is a gleaming white—let the game begin! But even these seemingly innocent groundskeeping chores can sometimes have a competitive intent, as teams seek every last advantage over the opposition. Weak home-team outfield defense? Let the grass grow long. Home team populated with good bunters? Add so much paint to the lines that they form a raised barrier, keeping bunted balls in fair territory.

Mudball

Fresh from the factory, baseballs are too slick and shiny for game use. The solution? Lena Blackburne Baseball Rubbing Mud, carefully extracted from a zealously guarded secret location along the Delaware River in New Jersey. Able to give pitchers and players a better grip without turning the ball brown, and thankfully odorless, the mud is carefully applied to every baseball used in every game. Here, Umpire Eric Gregg does his pregame duty.

The Old-Fashioned Way

In an age of year-round training, in-depth statistical analysis, and computers in the clubhouse, some things about baseball never really change. One is the lineup card, scrawled after long rumination before each game by the manager and typically a mess of cross-outs and second thoughts by game's end. Here, longtime manager Sparky Anderson faces the new day's challenges.

Don't Touch

Surrounded by the tools of their trade, Ichiro Suzuki (#51) and his American League teammates await the start of the 2002 All-Star Game in Milwaukee. For Ichiro, the care of his glove—a handmade model that he oils daily, in the foreground here—is an important responsibility. Nor does he let teammates put their hands inside it. "If someone does, that bothers me," Ichiro admits. "Or if the glove is on the bench and someone sits on it, that *really* bothers me."

Getting There

There's a lot of downtime before the game begins. Players stretch, run a few lackadaisical wind sprints, take some batting practice, and do their fair share of nothing. But a lot of preparation for a game is internal, as the athletes strip away all outside distractions and prepare themselves for the intense focus that is necessary to play baseball at the highest possible level. They may not look like it, but they're working!

Lumberyard

The great Honus Wagner said that the best bat he ever used was a heavy old table leg. Today's bats are precision-tooled—but even so, every hitter has his own personal relationship with his war club. "When I am out for a homer," Babe Ruth said, "I try to make mush out of the solid ash bat handle." Demurring, Tony Gwynn said: "The tendency is to squeeze the bat. Squeeze the sawdust out of it. I wait and wait, and let the ball get right on top of me and just swing with a loose grip."

Almost Everything You Need

The weapons of a baseball war await the combatants and the beginning of the game. Caps, batting gloves, and bats are all carefully labeled with the players' numbers to avoid any in-game confusion. But that doesn't mean that there's no sharing. Every year the story emerges of a slump-ridden player who borrows a teammate's club and uses it to win an important game.

Entering a New World

There's nothing like the feeling of emerging from the dark interior of the stadium into the vast, colorful expanse of the stands and the field below. The field seems an almost electric green, and the noise from the crowd makes your heart pound. Every game, it's like stepping into a gigantic theater where you don't know what you're about to witness—but you're always sure it will be something exciting.

The Manager's Plight

"I'm as nauseous as I've ever been. I have a terrible headache. My head is pounding. I feel like throwing up and I'm having trouble swallowing. And the beauty of it is, you want to feel like this every day," wrote St. Louis Cardinals manager Tony La Russa of the joys and tribulations of managing a major-league team. He must have been telling the truth, for by the end of the 2007 season, La Russa had had that experience more than 4,400 times.

Heart of the Rockies

Strong and serious, Don Baylor was a natural to be the first manager of the expansion Colorado Rockies, enlisted to turn a collection of prospects and fading veterans into a winning team. "I don't hold these guys to any higher standard than I held myself to as a player," he said. In 1993, their first year, the Rockies set a record for wins for an expansion club (sixty-seven), and just two years later, they were the National League's wild card, making by far the fastest trip to the postseason of any expansion team in history.

"And the Home of the Brave..."

"The Star-Spangled Banner" has been sung at major-league games for more than a century, far longer than it's been America's national anthem. "It is well to remember," wrote Herbert H. Paper in the Cincinnati *Enquirer* in 1989, "that a Martian observing his first baseball game would be quite correct in concluding that the last two words of the National Anthem are: PLAY BALL!"

The Curtain Goes Up

Having departed Montreal, headed south, and changed their name, the Washington Nationals welcome baseball back to the District of Columbia after a hiatus of more than thirty years. Here, the veteran Livan Hernandez pitches on Opening Day at RFK Stadium, April 14, 2005. The Nationals beat the Diamondbacks, 5–3, that day, and went on to post a very respectable 81–81 record for the season.

Play Ball

Game time at last. "I do love the baseball that is in the heads of baseball fans," wrote Stan Isaacs in *Newsday*. "I love the dreams of glory of ten-year-olds, the reminiscences of seventy-year-olds. The greatest baseball arena is in our heads, what we bring to the games, to the telecasts, to reading newspaper reports."

The Donut

When they're in the on-deck circle, ballplayers often swing a weighted bat—or even multiple bats—so that when they step up to the plate their unburdened bat will feel so light that it will whip through the strike zone. Some have argued that using a weight beforehand actually slows the swing at the plate, but no matter. Most players—including Paul Molitor here—use a batting donut, a relatively recent innovation.

Louisiana Lightning

"Ron Guidry is not very big, maybe 140 pounds, but he has an arm like a lion," said broadcaster and master of the mixed metaphor Jerry Coleman. Feline limbs aside, Guidry was an exceptional pitcher for some of the great Yankee teams of the 1970s and '80s. Not quite reaching six feet in height (and actually weighing around 160), he somehow still unleashed a devastating fastball-slider combination to dominate hitters. In 1978, his career year, Guidry went 25–3 with a 1.74 ERA, and helped lead the Yankees to their second consecutive championship.

Brett Bunter

With 538 bunt and other infield hits among his lifetime total of 2,375 hits, Brett Butler, a classic leadoff man, was one of the best bunters of his—or any—generation. As any number-one hitter should do, he made things happen, getting on base (1,129 career walks), stealing (558 SBs), and messing with the pitcher's concentration. Add a .290 lifetime batting average, as many as 14 triples in a season, and 1,359 runs scored, and you have one of the most underappreciated stars of the 1980s and '90s.

The Move

When a pickoff works, it's a thing of beauty, a trick played on the opposing teams and the fans alike. Without warning, the pitcher (in this case, Pedro Martinez) whirls and fires, the runner plunges into the dirt, the first baseman applies the tag, the umpire's arm flies upward, and the crowd howls. As Eric Neel put it so evocatively on ESPN.com: "As it is with a good changeup, or with a good bluff at the poker table, the trick is to have no trick, to show not tell, leave no trace of your intentions. You want a quiet body, a still face, and a shrouded heart."

Young All-Timer

Long before he became a lightning-A-Rod with the Yankees, Alex Rodriguez was putting up some of the best numbers of all time as a young shortstop with the Seattle Mariners. The earlier you prove you can hit major-league pitching, the better your chances of becoming a superstar—and as a twenty-year-old (turning twenty-one midseason) in 1996 A-Rod hit .358, with 54 doubles, 36 home runs, 141 runs scored, and 123 RBI. Oh, and he played shortstop brilliantly, too.

Rambling Rose

Think what you will of Pete Rose, no one could ever doubt that he gave everything he had every moment he was on the field. The flying hair, missing helmet, and full-tilt aggressiveness are indelibly engraved in the minds of anyone who saw him play. "Sliding headfirst is the safest way to get to the next base, I think, and the fastest. You don't lose your momentum," said Pete, in his inimitable fashion. "And there's one more important reason I slide headfirst: It gets my picture in the paper."

Put It in the Book

Giants Manager Dusty Baker and his team celebrate a 1994 victory. The stresses of being a manager have to be experienced to be believed. (Hall of Fame manager Walt Alston, hearing that his ex-player Gil Hodges had been chosen to manage the Washington Senators, said, "I'm happy for him, that is, if you think becoming a big-league manager is a good thing to have happen to you.") But there are day-to-day rewards, not the least of which is a hard-earned win, which enables a manager to get up the next day and do it again.

One for the Phans

Most baseball teams have mascots that seem charmingly old-fashioned in a digital age. But neither Billy the Marlin, Dinger the Dinosaur, nor Wally the Green Monster have the charm of the Philly Phanatic—no surprise, since he was created by the great Jim Henson of Muppets fame. Since his debut in 1978, the Phanatic—riding around the field on an ATV, harassing opposing players, keeping young fans happy—has become perhaps the most famous mascot in all of sports.

The Fans' Mantra

"We Believe," proclaim fans at Shea Stadium. Such loyalty is what keeps bringing fans back to any ballpark. Whether they're at Yankee Stadium watching a team that has won nine consecutive division titles or cheering an expansion team that will be lucky to avoid 100 losses, fans always believe that this game, this moment, will be the one that gives them something new, something exciting, something they will never forget. And, remarkably often, they're right.

Leadership

Joe Carter had charisma to burn, but something more as well: intensity, drive, a feel for the big moment. Right at the beginning of Carter's career, the historian Bill James recognized this. "Leadership is a hard thing to define," James wrote, "but Carter was a player who gave the opposition *nothing*. If he hit a single and you didn't hustle in after it, he'd take second. If the team was ten runs behind, he'd try twice as hard." In 1992 and 1993, when Carter led the Toronto Blue Jays to their first championships, the world learned what James and others had recognized years before.

Trick Pitcher

They're as rare as a blue moon in modern-day baseball, but throughout the game's long history knuckleballers have thrived by throwing the floating, darting pitch that drives batters—and catchers—crazy with its unpredictability. Here Tom Candiotti, who rode the knuckler to a sixteen-year career, unleashes one. "There are two theories on hitting the knuckleball," said renowned hitting expert Charlie Lau. "Unfortunately, neither of them works."

Stee-rike!

Umpire Eric Cooper rings up an emphatic call on Bobby Higginson. Nothing grinds a ballplayer's gut like striking out, though that fine player Bobby Bonds, an expert at the act (his season high was an astonishing 189), took a more philosophical approach. "If you get 200 hits a season, you're going to hit .333, and you'll still have 400 outs," he famously said. "I don't see why you have to run down to first base every time to make an out."

Thome Time

Cleveland Indians fans laud slugger and hometown hero Jim Thome in a photo from 1997, when Thome hit 40 homers and knocked in 102 runs. That was also the year when the Indians captured the American League Central, beat the Yankees in five games in the A.L. Division Series, overcame the Baltimore Orioles in six in the A.L. Championship Series, and took the upstart Florida Marlins to a seventh game before falling short in the World Series.

Bat on Ball

"The hardest thing to do in baseball is to hit a round baseball with a round bat, squarely," said Ted Williams. It's easy to tell this when you see even the greatest hitters—including Ted himself, every once in a while—struggle for days or weeks to make contact. Succeeding here is the Rangers' Hank Blalock, who in his first full season (2003) hit .300 with 29 home runs and 90 RBI.

On His Toes

All concentration, Ryne Sandberg—a superb ballplayer throughout his career with the Cubs—waits to see where the ball will go next. (That's fellow Hall of Famer Ozzie Smith behind him.) Sandberg was one of those players who always seemed a move or two ahead of the competition. "It was all about doing things right," Ryno said of his career. "If you played the game the right way, played the game for the team, good things would happen."

The New Mick?

Carlos Beltran (born in Manati, Puerto Rico) is a player who signals both the increasing Latin influence on baseball and the reappearance of a rare kind of player: the speedy slugger. While a generation ago, most players were either big, hulking power hitters (the Harmon Killebrew/Boog Powell model) or little speedsters (Maury Wills/Luis Aparicio), Beltran—like Mickey Mantle before him—combines the traits of both. In 2004, for example, playing for both the Kansas City Royals and the Houston Astros, Beltran slammed 38 home runs while also stealing 41 bases and playing one of the most demanding of all positions, center field.

The Wizard

How good a fielder was Ozzie Smith, shown here forcing out the Reds' Barry Larkin at second base? This book could be filled exclusively with spectacular examples of his fielding prowess—and all the text could be taken from encomiums given to him by his grateful pitchers. Such as this one from his Hall of Fame teammate Gaylord Perry: "Ozzie Smith was a great shortstop.... I was always hoping they would hit the ball his way because I knew then that my trouble was over."

Safe . . . or Out?

Umpire Jim McKean prepares to make the call. ("Gentlemen, he was out because I *said* he was out," said pioneering ump Bill Klem, voicing every umpire's credo.) Each ump has his own distinct style, manner, and temperament, but all, opined *Time* magazine in 1961, "should combine the integrity of a Supreme Court judge, the physical agility of an acrobat, the endurance of Job, and the imperturbability of Buddha."

The Man Behind the Plate

The runner heads home. The throw wings its way in from the relay man and thuds into the catcher's mitt. There's a slide, a cloud of dust, a moment of waiting, and then the umpire's call: SAFE! No position on the field is more demanding, yet you hardly get noticed except when you fail, as the Los Angeles Dodgers' Todd Hundley did here. Hall of Fame backstop Bill Dickey said it best: "A catcher must want to catch. He must make up his mind that it isn't the terrible job it is painted, and that he isn't going to say every day, 'Why, oh why, with so many other positions in baseball, did I take up this one?'"

Conference Call

No one on the baseball field works harder than the catcher (in this case, the Cincinnati Reds' Jason LaRue). Not only does he have to squat in foul territory the whole game, he also has to call the pitches, chase after them when they're wild, grovel in the dirt to block them, and be prepared to spring up and sprint after a bunt or squib hit at any moment. And then he has to take some of the blame if a pitcher falls apart! How to handle the strain? "You have to play with pride—for the game and for yourself," said longtime catcher Sandy Alomar, Jr. "You have to go out and give a major-league effort."

Killing Time

The Atlanta Braves' Chipper Jones keeps busy during a pause in the action. Whether it's flipping sunflower seeds, checking out the crowd, playing practical jokes on teammates, or ragging on the umpire, ballplayers keep themselves entertained during the inevitable delays that punctuate every game. "Baseball is a slow, sluggish game, with frequent and trivial interruptions, offering the spectator many opportunities to reflect at leisure upon the situation on the field," wrote Edward Abbey. "This is what a fan loves most about the game."

On the Lookout

"Nobody knows his name, but everybody recognizes him," wrote Roger Angell in *Five Seasons*, "for he is a figure of profound almost occult knowledge, with a great power over the future. He is a baseball scout." From the early days of big-league baseball, teams have employed experts to study opposing teams and search out prospects. Today, the job description includes using laptop computers, cell phones, and radar guns, but at heart it hasn't changed in generations.

Beware of Low-Flying Burgers!

A vendor prepares to unleash a volley of in-game snacks at Dodger Stadium. Certainly the most famous ballpark vendor of all time was Roger Owens, who began work in the Los Angeles Coliseum in 1958, the year the Dodgers moved west, and then followed the team to Chavez Ravine. So stylishly did Owens wing bags of peanuts and other comestibles (he could throw two bags thirty rows away simultaneously with pinpoint accuracy) that he ended up as a regular guest on *The Tonight Show* and various game shows, and even appeared in movies.

The Tactician

With both the Kansas City Royals and the St. Louis Cardinals, Whitey Herzog developed a reputation as a brilliant strategist and an uncompromising boss. He artfully constructed his teams to suit their ballparks and never hesitated to get rid of even popular players who didn't follow his code. "Herzog is too smart to believe in building a ball club by trading, or building a ball club from free agency or building a ball club out of the farm system," wrote Bill James during Herzog's reign. "He believes in building a ball club out of *ballplayers*."

Easy Living?

People who've never played major-league baseball have no idea of the demands it places on its stars. ("Baseball gives you every chance to be great. Then it puts every pressure on you to prove that you haven't got what it takes," Joe Garagiola once said. "It never takes away that chance and it never eases up on the pressure.") The only solution, for players like Bobby Abreu, is to relax, take a deep breath, and enjoy themselves when they can.

Be Vewwy Vewwy Quiet!

With all the prearranged signs and secret signals that pass between ballplayers—and remain mysterious to onlookers—in every game, sometimes one comes along that is particularly intriguing. What was Bobby Bonilla planning here? A practical joke? A steal of home? Or, like Elmer Fudd in all those classic Bugs Bunny cartoons, was he merely hunting wabbits? We'll never know.

Let's See *You* Do That!

As if being the most brilliant shortstop of his generation wasn't enough, Ozzie Smith was also able to do flips. At first he would show his moves only in private, but finally, the San Diego Padres (his team at the time) prevailed upon him to try them in public. After word of his talent got out, Ozzie recalled, "The fans went nuts. I really had no choice on Opening Day. I had to do it." The tradition continued when he was traded to the Cardinals—and even included one last flip on September 28, 1996, during Ozzie Smith Appreciation Day.

End of the Road?

In 1980, his first season with the Houston Astros, Nolan Ryan had what was for him a bad year. Thirty-three and with a lot of mileage on his right arm, he went only 11–10, threw only 4 complete games (down from 17 in 1979, his last year with the California Angels), and saw his strikeout total dip to 200 from 341 just three years earlier. Was his career coming to an end? In a word, no. The amazing Ryan would pitch for another fourteen years, totting up 146 more wins, adding an astounding 2,600 or so additional strikeouts to his record-shattering total, and marching directly into the Hall of Fame.

Wardrobe Malfunction

Something happened in the 1970s that is unlikely ever to be repeated: The designers of baseball uniforms decided that fans wanted to see great players from Willie McCovey to Willie Stargell to Dave Winfield (and their teammates, too) decked out in sunny yellows, fiery reds, and incandescent greens. Even the grim-visaged Dave Parker, here in one of his Pirate uniforms, had to try to intimidate the opposition while looking a lot like a dandelion.

One Big Blur

Has there ever been a more intimidating pitcher than Randy Johnson? He seemed to emerge directly from batters' worst nightmares: a gawky six-foot-ten lefty with an impossible-to-read motion and a 100-mph fastball. Worse, especially early in his career, neither batters nor even Johnson himself had any idea where his pitches were going. With Seattle in 1992, for example, he pitched 210 innings and struck out 241 batters... while walking an astonishing 144 men, plunking 18 more, and throwing 13 wild pitches. Batters' hearts must have been in their mouths every time they approached the plate.

The Bulldog

Mike Flanagan was a productive pitcher for the Baltimore Orioles for more than a decade. Winning twenty-three games and the Cy Young Award in 1979, he led the O's to the World Series. But among his teammates, he was best known for his sense of humor and ability to pin memorable nicknames on others. It was Flanagan, for example, who dubbed the aging Jim Palmer "Cy Old" and flaky reliever Don Stanhouse "Stan the Man Unusual." Said teammate Ken Singleton of Flanagan, "He's calm and invisible and lays back and, then, for about ten seconds, he's hilarious."

Think Quick

What's it like to face Randy Johnson, or Nolan Ryan, or any pitcher with a 90-mph fastball? For most of us, it's unimaginable. But for professional hitters, it's all in a day's work... as long as you have nerves of steel and the reflexes of a cat. Here, as if enduring the bumps and bruises of his life as a catcher wasn't enough, Javier Lopez has to duck out of the way of an errant pitch.

A Vision in Red

Buddy Bell starred for the Cleveland Indians at a time when baseball's fashion arbiters went temporarily color blind, but it wasn't his fault. Playing always with focus and enthusiasm, he compiled near Hall of Fame–quality numbers, including 2,514 hits in an eighteen-year career. "I had a lot of fun playing baseball," he wrote after he retired in 1989. "There were times in certain games when I was so thrilled to be part of the competition that I wished the game would never end." Watching him, it was easy to tell.

What Makes a Hall of Famer

Hustle. Hard work. Never giving up. And talent, of course. Dave Winfield had all these and more. While never the dominant player in his league, he compiled 15 years with 20 or more home runs, eight 100-plus RBI seasons, and a lifetime total of 3,110 hits, even while overcoming a serious injury that caused him to miss an entire midcareer season. Here, past the age of forty, he still exhibits the grit and energy that characterized his whole career.

Let Me Out of Here!

When Craig Biggio moved out from behind the plate, part of the reason was to preserve his health—catchers' careers are shorter on the whole than any other position player's. It may not have been the smartest move to land at second base, however: Between the twisting motion required on many plays, and the ever-present risk of injury from a take-out slide, second-sackers spend more than their share of time on the disabled list as well. Here, Biggio's gymnastic ability helps him escape from the barreling body of the Phillies' Mark Parent.

Ryno

Hall of Fame second baseman Ryne Sandberg wasn't the flashiest star around, but he had no weaknesses. He won the N.L. Gold Glove every year from 1983 through 1991 and the Silver Slugger at the position seven times. Add to that as many as 54 stolen bases and 40 home runs in a season, 10 All-Star appearances, and an M.V.P. Award, and all he was lacking—like fellow Cubs Hall of Famer Ernie Banks—was a World Series championship.

The Dominator

By the time he came to Arizona in 1999, Randy Johnson had conquered his earlier control problems and become an overpowering pitcher. (He'd gone 39–15 the previous two seasons, striking out an amazing 620 batters in 457 innings.) With the Diamondbacks in '99, he posted 364 Ks, walked only 70, and won the Cy Young Award. But it never hurt him that a hitter stepping to the plate would remember the old, scatter-armed flamethrower, and wonder whether *this* might be the at-bat when one got away from the big lefty.

The Swing

Is there any easier act in sports than swinging a bat? Anyone can do it. The problem is doing it at the exact right instant and in the exact right spot to redirect a small white hardball that has arrived at 90 or even 100 miles per hour, sending it on a line away from the waiting gloves of any of eight men in the field, or perhaps even over a distant fence. It's a magnificent achievement, one that only a very few athletes can accomplish even once, much less three or four times in any one game. Here, Joe Carter, who redirected more than 2,000 hardballs for hits in his career, takes a healthy cut.

Soft Touch

"You don't walk off the island," is the famous line describing why players from the Dominican Republic tend to be free swingers. But it's also true, for nearly every major leaguer, that in this power-happy era you don't make the Show by bunting. It's not quite a lost art—as the Colorado Rockies' Willy Taveras and the New York Mets' Endy Chavez, among others, have shown—but fewer and fewer players ever attempt to bunt for a base hit these days. Here, future Hall of Famer Paul Molitor lays down a beauty.

On the Double

Eric Young throws to first to complete the double play, sending Eric Davis back to the dugout unhappy. There are few plays that are more satisfying to watch than a smoothly turned pivot over the second-base bag. "The poet or storyteller who feels that he is competing with a superb double play in the World Series is a lost man," opined author John Cheever. "One would not want as a reader a man who did not appreciate the finesse of a double play."

Bang Bang

Since an umpiring crew rotates from base to base each game, after an ump works home plate (obviously the most demanding job), he'll move on to the less challenging job at third for the next. Of course, he still may be called on to do more than indicate whether batted balls are fair or foul. Here, umpire Larry Young gets to exercise his "out" sign, and what an out sign it is.

Fiery

Philadelphia's Larry Bowa risks expulsion from a game, an outcome with which he was all too familiar. For those ballplayers with hair-trigger tempers, a close or blown call by an umpire is an almost unsupportable affront. The result of such temper tantrums is inevitable: They begin to color your reputation. "Every time I get on a show, like a radio show, it's, 'Well, today we have the fiery Larry Bowa,'" the emotional player lamented. "Why not use the word 'intense'? Or, 'a guy that likes to win'?"

"It Ain't Nothin' Till I Call It"

These immortal words of the Hall of Fame umpire Bill Klem have served as inspiration to every umpire since. Unfortunately, this philosophy has its detractors, especially among baseball managers. Here, the Los Angeles Dodgers' Davey Johnson expresses his displeasure after a call didn't go his team's way. But, in an outcome clear to all participants before Johnson even set foot outside the dugout, he lost the argument.

Too Many Men on the Field

Managers Joe Torre and Don Baylor mill around with umpire John McSherry after a hit-by-pitch in a Cardinals-Rockies game in 1994. For every true brawl on the baseball diamond, there are many comparatively peaceful incidents like this one, in which both sides get to squawk, everyone gets a bit of a breather, and then the game resumes with no harm, no foul.

Who, Me?!

The Giants' crestfallen J.T. Snow gets thrown out of the game. "Nobody ever says anything nice about an umpire, unless it's when he dies and then someone writes in the paper, 'He was a good umpire,'" ump Tom Gorman told Bob Uecker. "Oh, once in a while a player will tell you that you worked a good game behind the plate, but when that happens, it's always the winning pitcher who says it."

The Quiet Man

For a generation of baseball fans, it seemed like Steve Carlton was always around—and what he was usually doing was beating their team. ("Hitting against Steve Carlton is like eating soup with a fork," Willie Stargell once lamented.) But Lefty, always sensitive to criticism, rarely spoke to the media or fans during a 24-year career that ended with 329 wins. So he always seemed like an oddly remote figure—which was the way he liked it. "What I did on the field was the essence of what I am," Carlton said after his career was over. "Remember me like that."

The Quiet Man, Volume Two

Just like Steve Carlton, Eddie Murray kept his own counsel, rarely speaking with the press and keeping at arm's length from fans during his years in Baltimore and elsewhere. And just as Carlton seemed to gain strength and focus from his private ways, Murray did nothing but produce for the Orioles and other teams: 3,255 hits, 560 home runs, and 1,917 RBI. "I had to do what I had to do to make myself successful," Murray said in explanation for his distant manner, and his statistics bear him out.

I'm Old-Fashioned

Even in the rough-and-tumble 1970s, Graig Nettles seemed like a player from another time: the 1920s, perhaps, the years of Babe Ruth and Ty Cobb and others who played with joy and intensity and, frequently, unfettered aggressiveness. That made him a natural for Manager Billy Martin and the tumultuous Yankees of that era, who rampaged through the American League without making many friends. "When I was a little boy, I wanted to be a baseball player and join a circus," Nettles once said. "With the Yankees I've accomplished both."

Racing the Ball

The geometry of a play at the plate is one of the greatest marvels of baseball. No matter what their rooting interest, fans in the ballpark hold their breath and wish their eyes could focus independently. One would watch the runner (in this case, Bernie Castro of the Reds) flying around the bases, while the other would follow the flight of the ball home. Then both eyes would focus on the plate, as ball and runner and catcher (Damian Miller of the Arizona Diamondbacks) arrive in quick succession and the umpire signals safe or out. Only then do fans remember to breathe once again.

In Under the Tag

Dave Winfield slides in safely after one of the 3,000-plus hits of his twenty-two-year career. All those slides, all the bumps and bruises, all the facefuls of dirt—we don't fully appreciate what ballplayers endure playing a six-month season every single year for ten, fifteen, twenty, or even more years. You can only make it through if you maintain your intensity—something all the great ones, including Winfield, are able to do.

You Had a Bad Day

Minnesota Twins Manager Tom Kelly takes the ball from disgruntled pitcher Pat Mahomes while catcher Greg Myers looks on in this 1996 photo. The lot of the journeyman pitcher is one of the unsung stories of every baseball year: Mahomes went on to have some success (including an 8–0 season with the Mets), but in 1996 he went just 1–4 for the Twins, with a 7.20 ERA, before being traded to the Boston Red Sox. It's no wonder Kelly looked so unhappy.

High Fives

Ballplayers are a mix of tough, battle-tested competitors hardened by years of experience, careful tenders of their ever-cool attitudes, and enthusiastic little boys. Watching them celebrate a win, as these Cincinnati Reds are after a victory over the Houston Astros in 1996, most fans can be forgiven for wishing that *they* could be down there on the field, sharing in the camaraderie.

Three Superstars

What did you have when Gary Carter (facing camera), Tim Raines (#30), and Andre Dawson (#10) were together? Only 7,398 hits, 926 home runs, and 1,156 stolen bases—and, even more importantly, a joy of playing, of competition, that colored everything they did on the field. Only one, Gary Carter, made it to the Hall of Fame, but both Raines and Dawson were also superb players who will be remembered with affection by a generation of baseball fans.

Meet the Met

Bringing some of the charm of Charlie Brown to Shea Stadium, New York Mets mascot Mr. Met has entertained fans almost since the team's birth. In those early years, when the team routinely lost 100 or more games each season, Mr. Met was often the most professional figure in view. Back then, he was sometimes accompanied by "Lady Met" and three baby baseballs, but today he usually rolls solo.

Ivy-Rule Double

Every old ballpark has its quirks. Yankee Stadium has its short right-field porch, Fenway Park the Green Monster, and Wrigley Field—well, Wrigley has not only the Bleacher Bums but the famous ivy covering its outfield walls. Growing throughout the spring, it reaches its full glory in midsummer, when it's not rare for batted balls to disappear within its tangled vines. Here, Cubs outfielders Gary Matthews, Jr., and Sammy Sosa surrender to the foliage.

Just Relax

Jose Cruz, Jr. (center), Ken Griffey, Jr., and a pair of Seattle Mariners teammates enjoy a light moment in the dugout. (Nor do they seem to be very concerned about possible "objects leaving the playing field.") Some fans, especially those of struggling teams, are annoyed by seeing players smiling or joking. How can they not care? But in truth, the only way that ballplayers can survive a grueling six-month season is by learning to deal with tension. No matter how much each game means, if you don't know how to relax, your play will suffer.

Stopper Style

The idea of growing old-fashioned styles of facial hair—twirly mustaches, muttonchop sideburns—originated with 1970s Oakland A's owner Charles Finley, who offered each player a $300 bonus for complying. For some players, the look that resulted became their public image forever, none more so than closer Rollie Fingers, whose handlebar mustache made him one of the most familiar faces in baseball. And his 341 career saves and three consecutive championships with the A's (1972–74) earned him selection to the Hall of Fame.

It's Around Here Somewhere

Craig Biggio keeps track of his glove, which was a bigger challenge for him than for most other great players. Very few stars switch positions midcareer, and hardly any do it twice—but Biggio did: He came up in 1988 as a catcher (and played more than 400 games behind the plate); moved to 2B in 1992, playing eleven seasons there and winning four Gold Gloves; and then switched *again*, to center field, in 2003. Despite this shuffling, Biggio never stopped hitting: In 2007 he became the twenty-seventh player to reach the magical milestone of 3,000 hits.

The Eyes Have It

What a strange life professional baseball players lead. Every move they make is scrutinized, not only by fans and sportswriters, but by the long, unforgiving lenses of the media's cameras. That is far truer today—the era of ESPN and twenty-four-hour sports talk—than it was even a couple of decades ago. Ballplayers' lives are a true Truman Show—and if sometimes they act like they're tired of it, it should come as no surprise.

Turnabout Is Fair Play

A familiar sight to ballplayers of the 1970s and '80s: Future Hall of Famer Rod Carew behind the lens. "At home, especially during my years with the Angels," he wrote after his career, "my tripod and cameras were always set up at the end of the dugout ready to peek into the eyes of Gene Mauch or record the amazing raw power of the likes of Reggie Jackson, Don Baylor, or Nolan Ryan."

Interrogation

The baseball manager's lot is not an easy one. Not only does he have to contend with in-game strategy, bad luck, injuries, the egos of temperamental stars, and a dozen other daily challenges—he then has to justify what he does to a procession of story-hunting journalists, as San Francisco Manager Dusty Baker is doing here. And then he has to do it again the next day.

Joaquin

Joaquin Andujar never quite achieved the heights predicted for him. Passionate, emotional, and possessed of a hair-trigger temper, he created many of his own roadblocks. ("I win or I die," he once said.) The Houston Astros shuttled him back and forth from the starting rotation to the bullpen for years before shipping him to the St. Louis Cardinals, where he blossomed briefly into one of the league's best starters. The peak of his career came in 1982, when he went 2–0 with a 1.35 ERA in the Redbirds' World Series victory over the Milwaukee Brewers.

Granting the Fans' Wish

In 1997, after years of debate, baseball owners decided to institute a limited schedule of regular-season interleague games—memorialized by the logo reproduced here. While some objected to the move, the Seattle Mariners' Ken Griffey had this to say: "Anytime you play against a Barry Bonds or a Tony Gwynn you always do your best. There are friendly bragging rights to be won. Interleague play is good for baseball."

The Main Event

Of all the games bringing teams together in interleague play, none attract the attention—or the buzz—of those pitting the Yankees against the Mets. Every series between the two teams feels like a mini–World Series, something that drives their managers to distraction. Through 2006 the Yankees (a superb team every year since interleague matchups began) had won about two out of every three games against the upstart Mets. Here, the Bombers' Alex Rodriguez is at the plate, and the Mets' catcher is Paul Lo Duca.

Battle by the Bay

While some interleague games pit teams with no regional or competitive rivalry, others bring a special gleam to fans' eyes. One such is the confrontation between the neighborhood rivals San Francisco Giants and Oakland A's. The teams previously met during the brief (and interrupted) Earthquake Series of 1989, but now they face off every year. Here, the A's Jason Giambi swings while the Giants' Scott Servais hopes the ball reaches his glove.

One Brief, Shining Moment

So often, young pitchers appear on the scene like comets, lighting up the sky and capturing the public's attention. Mark Fidrych in 1976. Fernando Valenzuela in 1981. Dwight Gooden in 1985. And Kerry Wood in 1998, when as a 21-year-old fireballer he went 13–6, struck out an astonishing 233 men in 167 innings, led the Chicago Cubs to the postseason, and won the Rookie of the Year Award—as well as the hearts of fans at Wrigley Field. Sadly, Wood's career has been derailed by arm injuries that have allowed him to pitch 200 innings in a season just twice in his career.

The Global Game

Seattle Mariners fans spell out "Ichiro" in Japanese to celebrate an appearance by the international sensation who took the A.L. by storm after his arrival in Seattle in 2001, lashing more than 200 hits in each of his first six seasons. But he was far from the only foreign-born player to leave a mark on America's Pastime in the 2000s. By 2006, 28 percent of major leaguers were born outside the U.S., the most ever. Not at all coincidentally, overall attendance rose to more than 76 million in 2006, also an all-time record.

Hit Machine

Any doubt that Japanese hitters could thrive against major-league power pitching was laid to rest with the spectacular arrival of Ichiro Suzuki in 2001. Quiet and unassuming, he proceeded to break the all-time record for hits in a season in 2004, when he finished with 262. "I'm not a big guy and hopefully kids could look at me and see that I'm not muscular and not physically imposing, that I'm just a regular guy," he told the *Seattle Post-Intelligencer* that season. "So if somebody with a regular body can get into the record books, kids can look at that. That would make me happy."

A Long, Rich History

Adolfo Domingo de Guzman Luque was a solid pitcher with the Cincinnati Reds and other teams from 1914 to 1935. Beside his skill (he won in double figures eleven times), longevity, and noble name, Dolf Luque boasted another notable attribute: He came from Cuba. Luque ("The Prince of Havana") was one of the first players to show that the Caribbean was a source of great baseball talent—though one that would remain virtually untapped until the 1960s. Here, some Club Cubano fans enjoy an afternoon at Shea Stadium.

Godzilla Rises

How big a star was Hideki Matsui back in his native Japan? There's a museum celebrating his life and career in the city of Nomi. Years before he signed with the Yankees, Matsui (a three-time MVP in the Japanese leagues) got to strut his stuff before American stars during Major League Baseball's 1996 tour of Japan. His signing in 2003 spurred a celebratory parade in Tokyo, and even today his every at-bat is scrutinized by dozens of media people and countless fans back home.

See You Again Soon?

When the World Champion Baltimore Orioles toured Japan in 1971, playing against the Yomiuri Giants and their magnificent slugger, Sadaharu Oh, it was truly a meeting of separate cultures. No more. By the time of the 1996 tour, when this photo of American managers (including Dusty Baker, Don Baylor, and Art Howe) and players exchanging jackets with their Japanese counterparts was taken, the Japan-to-America pipeline was already opening. Today, more than a dozen Japanese players are thriving in the majors, including such stars as Hideki Matsui, Ichiro Suzuki, and Daisuke Matsuzaka.

North of the Border

While most of the attention is paid to foreign-born players from Japan, Korea, Latin America, and the Caribbean, Canada has been a steady supplier to the majors for decades. The Hall of Fame pitcher Ferguson Jenkins is perhaps the nation's most prominent baseball export, but there have been other good ones, including Justin Morneau (shown here participating in the 2002 Futures Game). A native of British Columbia, Morneau burst into public view in 2006, when he hit .321, blasted 34 home runs, and drove in 130 for the Minnesota Twins—and won the Most Valuable Player Award.

Heaven-Sent

Players born in Mexico have appeared in the majors since Baldomero Melo "Mel" Almada broke in with the Boston Red Sox in 1933. But few have had the impact of Fernando Valenzuela, who emerged as a rookie superstar with the Los Angeles Dodgers. Utilizing a funky delivery and an unhittable screwball, he went 13–7 during the strike-shortened 1981 season, with a league-leading 11 complete games, 8 shutouts, and 180 strikeouts. "He did not play baseball," wrote Earl Shorris, "he expressed himself through the art of pitching."

Welcome to the U.S.

When Chan Ho Park, born in Kongju, South Korea, made a cameo appearance with the Los Angeles Dodgers in 1994, he became the first player from his country to make it in the big leagues. Park would win 14 games in 1997 and 15 in 1998. He also participated in a memorable feat that he probably leaves off his resume: On April 23, 1999, he gave up two grand-slam home runs to the Cardinals' Fernando Tatis not only in the same game, but in the same *inning*.

Desire

For many years, the Japanese Leagues guarded their players zealously, refusing to allow them to cross over to play in the United States. For Hideo Nomo, the solution was to threaten to retire—a ploy that eventually enabled him to sign with the Los Angeles Dodgers in 1995. Almost immediately, the twenty-six-year-old with the hard-to-read, storklike windup made an impact with the Dodgers, winning the 1995 Rookie of the Year Award and notching forty-three victories in his first three years with the team.

Adjustment Period

In 2007 Daisuke "Dice-K" Matsuzaka (right) became the highest-profile Japanese player to arrive in the major leagues in years. A superstar back home, he was the subject of fierce bidding among several teams before ending up with the Boston Red Sox. But life wasn't always easy for the big right-hander (shown here with his interpreter Sachiyo Sekigucho and the Sox' pitching coach John Farrell) at first. Even the baseballs—slightly larger than their Japanese counterparts—seemed unfamiliar. Still, no one ever doubted that Daisuke would thrive in the U.S., just as he had back in Japan.

Universal Language

You don't need to speak Japanese to understand the 95-mile-per-hour fastballs, devastating change-ups, and unusual "gyroballs" that Daisuke Matsuzaka unleashes from the mound. Dice-K's language of baseball was especially familiar to the great Ichiro Suzuki, who'd batted against him many times back in Japan. When asked if he looked forward to a rematch on American soil, Ichiro said, "I hope he arouses the fire that's dormant in the innermost recesses of my soul. I plan to face him with the zeal of a challenger."

International House of Baseball

The 2006 World Baseball Classic proved beyond a shadow of a doubt that the game has taken hold in countries across the world. But all the signs had been there years earlier, as the Los Angeles Dodgers' Manager Tommy Lasorda noticed when he surveyed his pitching staff in 1999. "For starting pitchers we have two Dominicans, one Italian, one Mexican, and one Japanese," he pointed out. "In the bullpen we have a Venezuelan, a Mexican, a guy from the United States, and a guy from St. Louis."

Pure Joy

Korean players celebrate a victory in the first World Baseball Classic, in 2006. A true Cinderella team, Korea—led by first-baseman Seung-Yeop Lee, who hit five homers and drove in ten runs—went 6–0 in the first two rounds of the series, before losing to eventual champion Japan in the semifinals. Sixteen countries from six continents and three Caribbean islands participated in the tournament. Proving the international reach of major-league baseball, most teams featured at least a few star players "borrowed" from the big leagues.

Superstar Pals

The United States didn't exactly distinguish itself at the World Baseball Classic. ("With Barely a Whimper, U.S. Exits Classic," was the *New York Times* headline after the team fell to Mexico, 2–1.) But for American stars like Chipper Jones, Ken Griffey, Jr., and Derek Jeter, the Classic was a chance to play beside superstars who were usually opponents, skip the rigors of spring training, and plan to do better next time.

Next in Line?

With 464 home runs through 2006, when he was just thirty-one, Alex Rodriguez seems poised to take a run at Barry Bonds's lifetime record for round-trippers. He might even approach Hank Aaron's amazing total of 2,297 runs batted in. As remarkable as any of these feats is the fact that, when he joined the New York Yankees in 2004, he agreed to move from shortstop (where he'd been a Gold Glove) to third base. The reason: The Yankees already had their own future Hall of Famer, Derek Jeter (background), at the position.

Dominican Force

Forty-five years ago, the Alou brothers—Matty, Jesus, and Felipe—were among the first players hailing from the Dominican Republic to break into the big leagues. By 2006 the number had swelled to 146, a full 12 percent of all major leaguers. And, with more and more teams scouting the island nation for talent, the number is likely to keep growing. Here, Carlos Febles (born in the town of El Seibo) and Juan Encarnacion (Las Matas de Farfan) meet at second base.

I Got It!

For all kids who ever grew up enamored with baseball, their first glove, ratty and threadbare from use, looms large in their memory—though not as large as the nostalgic sculpture created to stand beyond the left-field fence at Pac Bell Park (now AT&T Park), home of the San Francisco Giants, in 2000. This giant glove, weighing in at more than a ton, has its own colorful history: It was inspired by a mitt given to the father of Giants executive vice president Jack Bair when he was a child in the late 1940s.

Hope Springs Eternal

Every day, in every ballpark, fans come equipped with gloves, nets, and the hope that *this* will be the day that they snare a foul ball. How exciting is it when it happens? When future Hall of Famer Rickey Henderson caught a foul while sitting in the stands during a May 2007 game at AT&T Park in San Francisco, he refused to give it to a young fan nearby. "I said, 'You're not getting this ball. I always wanted to get a foul ball. This one's going on a shelf at home,'" Rickey admitted after the game. (He did, however, sign another ball for the fan.)

The Stadium of the Past?

The 1988 All-Star Game was played at Cincinnati's Riverfront Stadium (later renamed Cinergy Field). Built in 1970, Riverfront was a classic example of the giant, artificially turfed, cookie-cutter stadiums that dominated baseball from the 1960s through the 1990s. Thankfully, beginning with the revolutionary Oriole Park at Camden Yards, which opened in 1992, more than a dozen cities have built smaller, less traditional, grass-field ballparks. Cincinnati's replacement for Riverfront, the Great American Ball Park, came on the scene in 2003, and another cookie-cutter was no more.

The Superstar

Every so often a slugger comes along who compels every viewer's attention when he steps to the plate. The St. Louis Cardinals' Albert Pujols is the latest such player: His calm, confident demeanor, explosive swing, and extraordinary power combine to make him a pleasure to watch. In 2005, when this photograph was taken, Pujols hit .330 with 41 home runs and 117 RBI—typical numbers for a player who seems a lock to make the All-Star team every single year.

Different Strokes

As every All-Star Game does, the 1989 affair brought together players of great talent and vastly different styles. Here are ever-smooth and even-tempered Ozzie Smith; that fireplug of cheerful intensity, Tony Gwynn; and the relentlessly intense Will Clark. There were, however, three qualities that all three shared: an unquenchable desire to exceed expectations, a drive to make their mark on the game, and a fearsome desire to win.

Only the Fourth Musketeer Was Missing

Was there ever a better starting rotation? Young, talented, and self-confident, the Atlanta Braves' All-Star starters—Steve Avery, Tom Glavine, and John Smoltz—relax at the 1993 game. Avery went 18–6 that season, Glavine 22–6, and Smoltz 15–11. The only one to miss making the team was Greg Maddux—and all he did that year was win twenty games with a league-leading 2.36 ERA! Today, Glavine, Smoltz, and Maddux are all likely Hall of Famers.

It Takes Two Thieves

The extraordinary Rickey Henderson and Lou Brock enjoying a lighthearted moment at the 1990 All-Star Game. Brock, himself a six-time All-Star with the St. Louis Cardinals, owned the career stolen-base record of 938, until Rickey came along and broke it in 1991. By the time this photograph was taken, Henderson had already accumulated nearly as many career SBs as Brock did—yet Rickey still had a dozen years and about 500 stolen bases to go in his run.

Satisfaction

The Chicago White Sox' Magglio Ordonez celebrates a 2004 game-winning hit. Ordonez, who had averaged more than 30 home runs and 100 RBI in the previous five seasons, had little to crow about in his injury-plagued 2004, when he managed only 9 homers in little more than 200 at-bats. Not until 2006, when he slugged 24 home runs and again climbed over the 100-RBI mark with the Detroit Tigers, did Ordonez again become the feared hitter he'd once been.

The Perennial

Robin Yount first played shortstop for the Milwaukee Brewers in 1974, when he was just eighteen years old. Even as a teenager, he was an above-average hitter at his position, but as he drew closer to his prime he became something much more: a fine fielder and consistent .300 hitter who ended up with 3,142 hits, an MVP award, and a plaque in the Hall of Fame. Remarkably, though, he was selected to the All-Star team only three times. While there may always have been a couple of shortstops having better years, only a few in the history of baseball ended up with a greater career.

The Surgeon

"One thing anyone can go through is a slump," said Mike Piazza. "Unless you're Greg Maddux, it's going to happen to everybody." Such words of praise and respect were echoed by every player during the peak of Maddux's career, when he seemed to throw the ball exactly where he wanted to every game, even every pitch. His pitching style, wrote Michael Geffner in *Sporting News*, "is perfectly calculated and unrelentingly diabolical, striking suddenly, pitch after pitch, at the hitter's weakest points." With more than 300 wins and counting, he's an automatic first-ballot Hall of Famer.

Glove Happy

Batting gloves, omnipresent today, weren't always a fixture of the game. Historians pinpoint Bobby Thomson as the first man to sport them (in spring training of 1949), but it was the iconoclastic Hawk Harrelson of the Kansas City A's who first wore them in a regular-season game. Today, nearly everyone—including Troy Glaus, pictured here—uses batting gloves, and it's the players who don't (like Vladimir Guerrero and Moises Alou) who get noticed.

Vlad the Warrior

With a dwindling fan base, an unlikable ballpark, and money woes, it was hard to stand out as a member of the Montreal Expos in the 1990s. But Vladimir Guerrero figured out a way: by playing as well as the greatest sluggers in the game. Perhaps the best bad-ball hitter since Roberto Clemente, Vlad broke onto the scene in 1997, when he was just twenty-one, and since then has only continued to provide sterling defense and oft-spectacular offense, first for the Expos and more recently for the Los Angeles Angels of Anaheim.

Quiet Star

Despite a superb career, the hard-nosed Jeff Bagwell (here sliding safely into home) never got the attention he deserved. Between 1996 and 2003, he hit more than 30 home runs every year (over 40 three times), exceeding 100 RBI in seven of those seasons. Though injuries ended his career too soon, he still compiled 449 home runs, 1,529 RBI, 2,314 hits, and a .297 batting average. Bagwell was also a great teammate, said catcher Brad Ausmus: "He was a superstar-caliber player who really understood what every single player, regardless of their rung on the ladder, was going through."

Irrepressible

It's hard to find an on-field picture of Kirby Puckett in which he's not smiling. The man played his whole short career as if there was nothing on earth he'd rather have been doing, and his joy was infectious, spreading to the usually more solemn Andre Dawson (here at the 1990 All-Star Game) and anyone else in range of Kirby's grin. "I could see how much he loved playing the game of baseball," said teammate Bert Blyleven. "His enthusiasm rubbed off on all of his teammates, including me."

The Difference Maker

Some stars, simply through the force of their personality, change the spirit of any new team they join. The irrepressible Pedro Martinez, shown here pitching on Opening Day 2005, his first game with the New York Mets, is one such player. The Mets were coming off a 71–91 season in 2004 and looked like a lost team. In 2005, led by Pedro's 15–8 record and his endless energy and inspiration, they finished 83–79—and in 2006 they came within a game of the World Series.

Dusty, Barry, and Junior

San Francisco Giants Manager Dusty Baker (left) shares a light moment with Ken Griffey, Jr., and Barry Bonds at the 1997 All-Star Game. Bonds had already proven himself to be one of the finest players in baseball history, but for better or worse it was the ebullient Griffey (on his way to a season of 56 homers and 147 RBI) who'd become the face of the game. "I'd like to have his abilities for a day, but not his life," said teammate Jay Buhner of Junior. "Popular has its price, and he pays it every day."

Who Knew Why?

There were few more talented ballplayers in the game's history than Dick Allen (left, with Don Sutton at the 1972 All-Star Game), prodigious slugger for the Phillies, White Sox, and other teams in the 1960s and '70s. At a time when runs were far scarcer than they are today, he hit as many as 40 homers (30 or more six times) and ended his career with a .292 batting average. Yet he was a moody, often uncooperative player who once "retired" while leading the league in home runs with two weeks to go in a season. "It is a strange, sad business," wrote Roger Angell of Allen's tumultuous career.

Price of Fame

That's Andres Galarraga down there at the bottom of this photo, mobbed by autograph seekers, as all baseball stars are. The relentlessness of the pursuit has become greater and greater as signed balls, programs, and the like have become potentially valuable memorabilia. While some players have responded by keeping their distance from the public, others—like Galarraga—continue to allow the close contact that young fans in particular find so precious.

Leather Meets Spike

Slick-fielding Philadelphia Phillies second baseman Placido Polanco hangs in against the onrushing Marquis Grissom of the San Francisco Giants. An exciting fixture in baseball from its earliest days, the stolen base has always been controversial among students of the game. How much is an extra base worth when measured against a potential caught stealing, a lost baserunner, and an additional out? The debate has faded in recent years, as the explosion in home runs has resulted in a steady decline in steals.

Newly Minted

The baseball media machine has an unquenchable appetite. It's always looking for its next big thing, preferably in a major market—someone's face to plaster on magazine covers. In 2005 the New York Mets' David Wright became the latest major-league media star. Modest, well-spoken, photogenic, and extremely talented, Wright (only twenty-four during the 2007 season) has had to juggle his newfound celebrity and his leading role on a resurgent Mets team.

Workaholic

Fielding never seemed to come as easily to George Brett as hitting did. But he approached third base with the same work ethic and boundless enthusiasm as he did everything else. (He also brought self-awareness, once saying, "If I stay healthy, I have a chance to collect 3,000 hits and 1,000 errors.") But if he was outshone by such stellar glovemen as Graig Nettles, Buddy Bell, and Gary Gaetti, Brett never let the position defeat him—and even took home a Gold Glove in 1985.

No Secrets

By 1974, when this picture was taken—the year that Lou Brock stole a then-record 118 bases—everyone knew from the moment he reached first that he was thinking steal. As Brock himself pointed out, this made the job much harder. "If you aim to steal thirty or forty bases a year, you do it by surprising the other side," he said. "But if your goal is fifty to a hundred bases, the element of surprise doesn't matter. You go even though they know you're going to go. Then each steal becomes a contest, matching your skills against theirs."

Hearing the Hoofbeats

The New York Yankees' Ruben Sierra leads the cavalry in this late-career shot from 2003. In the end, it nearly took a team of horses to drag Sierra off the field: He made his first big-league appearance in 1986 as a highly touted prospect for the Rangers... and two decades later, despite a run of serious injuries and conflicts with managers, he was still playing. His nine-team journey resulted in 2,152 career hits and 306 home runs, but Sierra himself realized that he'd been capable of much more. "I always thought that I was going to be a Hall of Fame player," he lamented in 2007, "but it didn't happen that way."

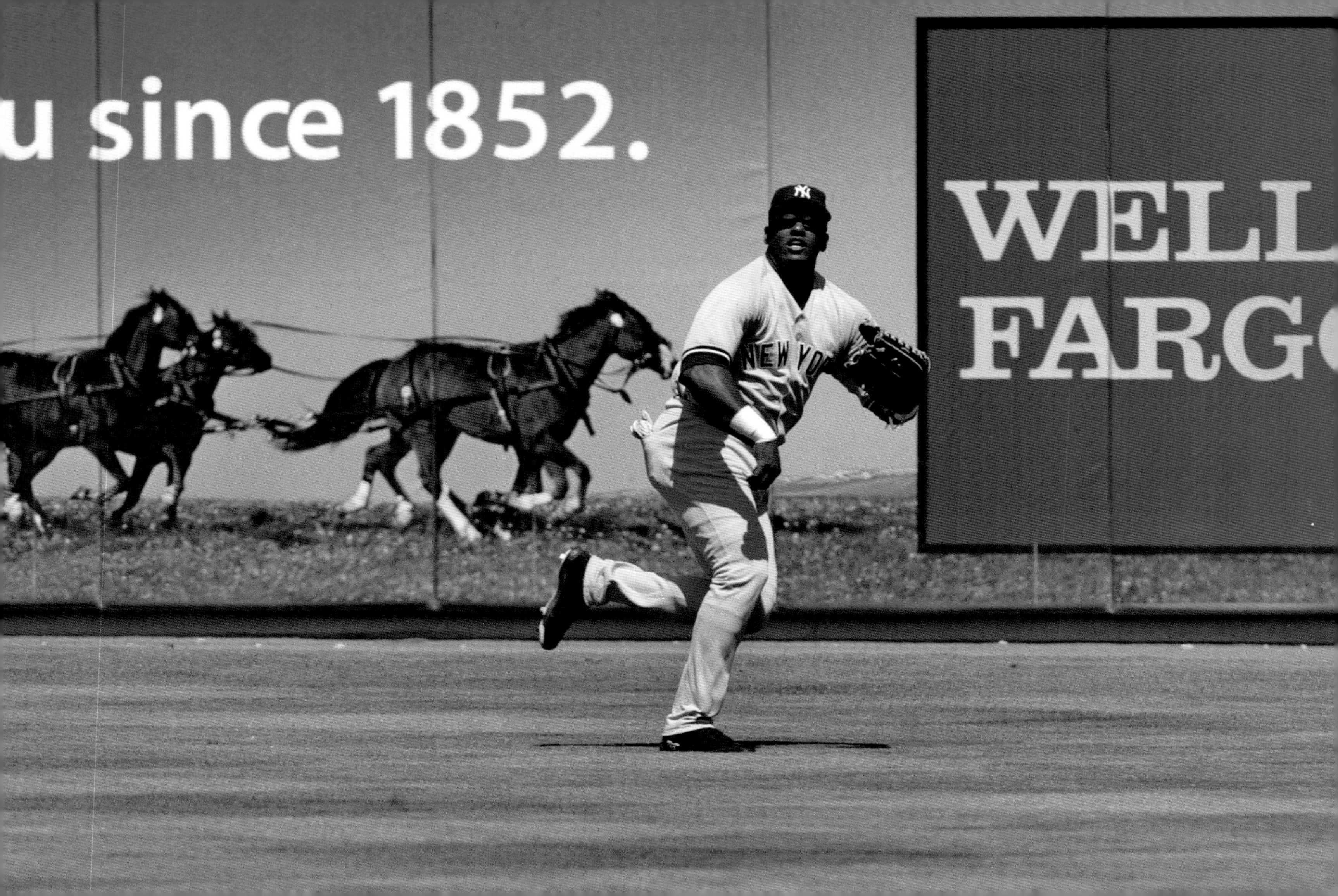
u since 1852.
WELL
FARG
NEW YORK

Desperado

Looking like nothing so much as an Old West gunslinger, Dennis Eckersley utilized a different kind of weapon: his right arm. Eckersley is one of the rare pitchers who spent years as a starter (he won twenty for the Red Sox in 1978) before making the transition to relief ace. His spectacular performances with the Oakland A's between 1988 and 1992 (as many as 48 saves and astonishing ERAs of 1.91, 1.56, and even 0.61) helped lead the team to three consecutive World Series appearances (1988–90) and the 1989 championship.

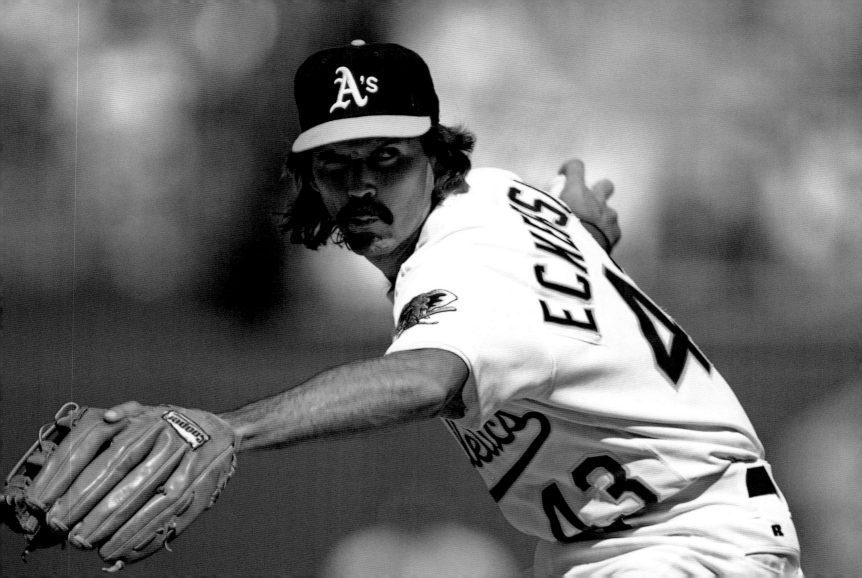

Reggie, Act One

Reggie Jackson left an indelible mark on baseball as a member of the tumultuous New York Yankees of the late 1970s, but before arriving in New York he was one of the leaders of the equally successful—and just as entertaining—Oakland A's, three-time repeat champions from 1972 through 1974. After missing the 1972 Series with an injury, Jackson began to establish his reputation as "Mr. October" with stellar performances in the A's subsequent championship runs.

Reggie, Act Two

It was in New York that the Reggie Jackson Three-Ring Circus truly came into its own. On a team filled with outsized personalities like Thurman Munson, Catfish Hunter, Graig Nettles, and manager Billy Martin, Reggie somehow became the face of the fractious Yankees. But the man himself, never at a loss for words, wasn't surprised. "I didn't come to New York to be a star," he said. "I brought my own star with me."

Reggie, Act Three

After leaving the Yankees following the 1981 season, Reggie Jackson was not quite ready to go gentle into that good night. While with the California Angels (and for his last season, Oakland), he added 138 home runs to his lifetime total, ending his career with 563. He also twice came within a game of making it one more time to the biggest stage of all, the World Series, where once again he might have become Mr. October.

Right Man, Wrong Time

Juan Marichal must be the greatest pitcher of all time who never managed to catch a break. Using a delivery that resembled, in the words of Roger Angell, "some enormous and dangerous farm implement," he won twenty or more games six times, with earned-run averages ranging from a minuscule 2.10 to a mere 2.76. So how many Cy Young Awards did he win? Counting carefully, the answer is: None. There was always somebody like Sandy Koufax or Bob Gibson around to post even better numbers.

The Waiting Game

Willie McCovey ended his long career with 521 home runs and 1,555 RBI, Hall of Fame numbers for sure. But he could have achieved even more. Arriving in the majors with the San Francisco Giants in 1959, he hit 13 homers and batted .354 in 192 at-bats. You'd think that would have earned him a full-time job, but for the next three years McCovey shared playing time with another Hall of Fame–caliber first baseman, Orlando Cepeda. With a few breaks, McCovey would likely have ended up with close to 600 round-trippers.

Portrait in Autumn

Nothing ever seemed to come easily for Carl Yastrzemski. As the Boston Red Sox' main man for nearly twenty years, he bore more than his share of the burden of the fans' busted dreams and broken hearts. Nor did he find it easy to live up to his Triple Crown year of 1967. Subsequently, in 1975 he failed to homer in the classic seven-game Series against the Cincinnati Reds, and in 1978 he made the last out in the memorable playoff game against the Yankees. "I loved the game, loved the competition, but I never enjoyed it," he said at the end of his career. "It was all work, all the time."

As We Remember Him

Tom Seaver pitched for four teams over his career. He threw his no-hitter as a member of the Cincinnati Reds and won his 300th game while with the Chicago White Sox. But to fans of a certain age, Tom Terrific will always be a member of the New York Mets. Joining the famously sad-sack team in 1967, he "made it clear at once that losing was unacceptable to him," as Roger Angell put it. Two seasons later, he went 25–7, led the Miracle Mets to their first World Championship, and pocketed the Cy Young Award.

Give Us the Willies

By 1978, when this photo was taken, a lot of water had passed under the bridge for these two superstars. A year earlier, Willie "Stretch" McCovey, forty years old, had made a deeply satisfying return to the San Francisco Giants, hitting twenty-eight home runs. And Willie "Pops" Stargell, thirty-eight, had an even bigger moment of glory ahead of him: the Pirates' heartwarming "We Are Family" World Championship of 1979.

The Eternal Flamethrower

Roger Clemens began his career, of course, with the Boston Red Sox in 1984. Pitching with the Houston Astros two decades later, a record seven Cy Young Awards and more than 300 wins behind him, he was still going strong, still throwing hard, still using his unparalleled intensity to dominate ballgames. "Everybody kind of perceives me as being angry," he once said. "It's not anger. It's motivation."

The Mood Changer

His career ended too soon. He died much too young, in 2006 at the age of forty-five. But Kirby Puckett (#34)—with (left to right) Edgar Martinez, Roberto Alomar, and Carlos Baerga—will always be remembered fondly by anyone who saw him play. "He never had a bad day. I don't care how bad things were going on or off the field, Kirby found a way to make you laugh," said slugger Frank Thomas. "He was a breath of fresh air in this game."

Self-Confidence

The San Francisco Giants' Jack Clark dives back into first as the Pittsburgh Pirates' Willie Stargell waits for the throw. The ever-intense Clark never quite fit the profile of a true superstar, but over an eighteen-year career he showed consistent home-run power and a knack for coming up big in the clutch. But it all came at a cost. "Jack wanted to win so bad he couldn't see straight," wrote Whitey Herzog, who managed Clark from 1985 through 1987. "Sometimes it made him a better player. Mostly, it just wound him up too tight."

Golden Age

Everyone has their favorite baseball eras. For many fans, the rough-and-tumble 1970s—which featured such cantankerous dynasties as the Oakland A's and the New York Yankees and such superb World Series as the Boston-Cincinnati 1975 classic—ranks with the game's peaks. This lineup of stars from the 1972 All-Star Game includes (left to right) Rod Carew (Twins), Bobby Murcer (Yankees), Reggie Jackson (A's), Dick Allen (White Sox), Carl Yastrzemski (Red Sox), Bobby Grich and Brooks Robinson (Orioles), and Bill Freehan (Tigers).

Birth of a Fan

In 1993 Ron Fimrite edited a lovely book called *Birth of a Fan*, in which writers ranging from Frank Deford to William Kennedy described their own earliest feelings about baseball. In her essay, "The Psychic Hat," Anne Lamott spoke some universal truths about the appeal of the game: "In some sentimental way, baseball lets you be a kid again, without being a fool," she wrote. "Everything is so green, and it's spring and then summer, and everything speaks of freshness and freedom."

Glove Affair

It's hard to know the details of this evocative shot of Chet Lemon with an old, obviously well-used glove. But anyone who ever owned—and treasured—a mitt can relate to the fond expression on Lemon's face. To avid ballplayers, the glove is more like a partner or a friend than an inanimate object: If you nurture it, care for it, and treat it with respect, it will never let you down.

The Brief History of Bo

"Baseball was fun when I was in college," Bo Jackson told *Sporting News* in 1989. "It's my job now." But though he claimed that he still enjoyed the major-league game, in truth it *seemed* like a job, and a struggle beyond anything he ever experienced as a star football player. In 1989, his best year with the Kansas City Royals, Bo hit 32 home runs, drove in 105 runs, and made the All-Star team. But he also struck out 172 times, and once pitchers learned to exploit the holes in his swing, his baseball career dwindled away.

About Time

In 1994 the National League celebrated its first All-Star Game victory since 1987—and what a game it was! The game ended, 8–7, in the bottom of the tenth inning when ten-time All-Star Tony Gwynn scored on a double by first-timer Moises Alou. National League Manager Jim Leyland (#10) celebrates with his team, while A.L. catcher Pudge Rodriguez looks disgusted that his league didn't win for the seventh time in a row.

Uncoiled

In real time at the ballpark, it happens as fast—and is as difficult to follow—as the strike of a rattlesnake. In slow motion on television, it looks almost lazy. Both views make it hard to understand how a batter swinging a thirty-ounce piece of wood can send a baseball soaring 400, or even 500, feet from home plate. In this photo, the powerful shoulders of slugger Jim Thome give at least a hint of the enormous energy unleashed in a swing. Thome had the move down pat, slamming thirty or more home runs ten times between 1996 and 2006.

Hard-Nosed

Solid as rock, square as a fireplug, Brian Downing—shown here crash-landing on home plate—looked little like a typical left-fielder and nothing at all like a leadoff hitter. But starting in the early 1980s, that's the role this converted catcher filled for Gene Mauch's Angels. And he was good at it, taking a walk, scoring runs, and always playing with exultant energy and intensity. He finished his twenty-year career with 275 home runs, 1,188 runs scored, and 1,073 RBI.

Gimlet Gaze

There's something about the eyes of a baseball slugger. They're more focused, more intense, than those of the rest of us. Perhaps it's a matter of natural selection: After all, a major-league player has to be able to pick out the speed, location, and spin of a small white sphere covering the sixty feet, six inches between the pitcher's mound and home plate at ninety or more miles per hour. Here, Jim Edmonds sizes up the competition.

Through the Looking Glass

Ever cool, reliever nonpareil Goose Gossage keeps an eye on the game. In his prime there was no closer more feared than the fireballing Goose. (And, unlike most of today's closers, you might have to face him in the eighth, or even the seventh, inning.) "Seventy-five percent of relief pitching is mental," he told *Sporting News*. "Sometimes I'll see a guy come up to bat against me and I can see he's already given up. I just say to myself, 'You're mine, sucker.'"

Storm Warnings

Talk about unsung heroes of the game! While everyone else, fans and players alike, scrambles for cover, the grounds crew ventures out onto the stormy field, braving lightning bolts, swirling winds, and billowing tarps to cover the infield—and increases the chance that more baseball will be played this day.

The Sparkplug

The Oakland A's Eric Byrnes uncharacteristically relaxes for a moment in the dugout. Byrnes is one of those rare players, beloved by fans, who always seems to play as if he's got a hornet trapped under his shirt, hitting, running the bases, and fielding with reckless abandon—even at the cost of his health. "I think every morning I wake up I'm a little dazed," he said once after an outfield collision. "For some reason, I'm used to hitting things with my head."

Home Away From Home

The clubhouse is where players' personal animosities sometimes boil over into brawls; where a frustrated pitcher may take out his anger on his locker door or an innocent sink; where a manager furious at lackadaisical play may turn over the refreshments table; where the elusive chemistry of a winning team can be lost. And it also can be the players' refuge—a place to work on tired, overused muscles (and eat candy)—as this one (the Oakland A's) clearly is.

Always Alone

Baseball is the most solitary of team sports, a game of individuals played in a group context. In the outfield, especially, every triumph is magnified—and so is every misstep. Al Bumbry, stalwart member of the powerful Baltimore Orioles teams of the 1970s and early 1980s, had what it took to do the job. Though never the dominant player on a team that featured such All-Stars as Frank and Brooks Robinson and Jim Palmer, Bumbry still managed to overcome serious injuries to hit over .300 three times and play all three outfield positions with skill and intensity.

Make 'Em Laugh

A generation ago, people went to the ballpark to see a ballgame. Today, in the era of instant gratification, fans need more—or, at least, stadium operators think they do. The result is a constant barrage of pop songs, trivia quizzes, rock videos, and contests between innings ... and even between pitches. Here, presented without explanation, is a trio of dancing baseball gloves. It must have taken extreme guts to climb inside those costumes and then perform in front of thousands of fans.

Long Road

Philadelphia Phillies manager Charlie Manuel (center), along with first-base coach Marc Bombard (#23) and bench coach Gary Varsho (#19), watches a 2005 game. Manuel was a marginal major leaguer for six years, accumulating a total of 384 at-bats and hitting .198. He then went off to Japan and thrived there, hitting as many as forty-eight home runs and earning the nickname "the Red Devil" for his aggressive play. Returning to the States, he worked his way up as a hitting coach before getting the chance to manage, first with the Cleveland Indians and then with the Phillies.

Start with a Bang

Few players had a rookie season to match that of Fred Lynn, with the Boston Red Sox. In 1975, when he was just twenty-three, he led the league in runs scored and doubles, batted a spectacular .331, and helped lead the Red Sox to the seventh game of the World Series. He had other good years (and one great one, 1979, when he batted .333 with 39 home runs), ending his career with a .283 batting average, 306 homers, and 1,111 RBI.

And Parallel Parking Is a Real Pain

A game-day tradition at AT&T Park in San Francisco: Fans jostling their pleasurecraft in McCovey Cove, hoping to scoop up a home run ball, preferably one slugged by Barry Bonds. One of the best things about the raft of new ballparks coming on line in the past decade or so is their idiosyncrasies: Every one has its nooks and crannies, warehouse walls, short porches, or jutting stands. But none is more distinctive—or features worse views of the field—than the Cove.

Hand, Glove, Dirt

Baseball is a long, sprawling, sometimes meandering game punctuated by moments of electrifying drama. Suddenly the ball is set free, a blurred white exclamation point against the vivid green of the grass. One fielder races after it, while the others head for the positions they've been taught to assume automatically. The batter speeds around the bases, the ball streaks in, there is the smack of cowhide against leather, dirt flies over outstretched hands, and an entire stadium holds its breath while waiting for the call. Safe... or out?

Chin Music

"When I knocked a guy down, there was no second part to the story," said the great Bob Gibson. And hitters, like Shawn Green (in this photo), still say that they take their lives in their hands every time they step up to the plate—not that it's always a bad thing. As Frank Robinson once said, "Pitchers did me a favor when they knocked me down. It made me more determined. I wouldn't let that pitcher get me out. They say you can't hit if you're on your back. But I didn't hit on my back. I got up."

He Always Had the Personality

Some great ballplayers just make you smile when you look at them. David Ortiz radiated strength, calm, and warmth, even when he was a young slugger struggling to establish himself with the Minnesota Twins. When he moved to Boston and helped the Red Sox end the decades-long Curse of the Bambino, the whole nation noticed what the Twins and their fans had long known: "He's like a superhero," said teammate Josh Beckett. "He's like that in real life, too, and I think that's why everything about him is so endearing."

Listen Up

Has any baseball manager ever loved to talk more than Tommy Lasorda? (Well, maybe Casey Stengel). The sportswriter's best friend, Tommy could always be counted on for a frank appraisal of the game, his team, and the best restaurants around town. ("When we win, I'm so happy I eat a lot. When we lose, I'm so depressed I eat a lot. When we're rained out, I'm so disappointed I eat a lot," he once acknowledged.) Between meals, that man sure could manage: In his two-decade career, Lasorda's Dodgers won 1,599 games, four pennants, and two World Series.

Think!

Kirby Puckett was never the most physically talented player out on the field. (In fact, if you saw him only in his street clothes, you would probably never guess that he was a professional athlete.) What made him such a remarkable success over the course of little more than a decade? He had all the usual driving forces behind a great career: intensity, self-confidence, an overwhelming desire to win. And Kirby had even more: He made up for his lack of great tools with pure baseball smarts.

En Garde!

While Bat Day has always seemed like a Bronx tradition—as this scene featuring longtime Yankees hurler Andy Pettitte demonstrates—it was baseball entrepreneur extraordinaire Bill Veeck who began the tradition as the owner of the hapless St. Louis Browns. Struggling to entice fans to come watch a team for whom a ninety-loss season was a moral victory, Veeck found himself offered six thousand bats by a company that was going bankrupt—and a promotion was born. "The most beautiful thing in the world is a ballpark filled with people," Veeck said, and Bat Day helps make it happen.

Playing the Angles

From the stands, fielding a baseball sometimes looks effortless. The pitcher unwinds and throws, the batter swings, the ball rockets across the diamond, is corralled by an infielder, and wings its way to first. The fact is, of course, that it isn't anywhere near that simple. So much of fielding depends on the almost superhuman reflexes and skills the players must possess: the ability to read the geometry of a batted ball and trust that proper mechanics will send it into the glove.

What, Me Buehrle?

If not quite an ace, Mark Buehrle has proven to be a solid, dependable starter for the Chicago White Sox—and sometimes much more. Pitching well over two hundred innings a year, winning sixteen or more games most seasons, he's a workhorse. But it was the briefest appearance of Buehrle's career that may have been the most memorable: the one-third of an inning he pitched to nail down the White Sox' agonizing, fourteen-inning victory over the Astros in Game Three of what turned out to be the Sox' four-game Series sweep in 2005.

Red-Faced

A portrait in dejection, the St. Louis Cardinals' Jim Edmonds ponders what went wrong after an unsuccessful at-bat. It's a baseball cliché that even the best players fail seven times out of ten (really, closer to six and half times), but it's also true that no sport is more filled with individual failure than this one. Even the greatest superstars don't always come through in the clutch. Babe Ruth, the biggest star of them all, batted .118 in one World Series (1922) and ended another with an ill-advised caught stealing (1926)!

Middle of the Action

Baseball is wonderful both for its possibilities—on any day you can see something you've never seen before—and for its familiarity. It doesn't matter what season, game, or even player is pictured here. Every baseball fan can visualize what's happening: the race around the bases, the hard slide into third, the runner popping to his feet, instantly locating the ball and making the split-second decision whether to head for home.

The Intimidator

One in a long line of flame-throwing relief pitchers, Rob Dibble, with a 100 mph fastball and the uncompromising personality to match, put together a spectacular season in 1990. Setting up closer Randy Myers, he posted an 8–3 record with a 1.74 ERA, 11 saves, and an awe-inspiring 136 strikeouts in 98 innings pitched. He then threw 5 no-hit innings (with 10 Ks) in the League Championship Series and another 4.2 scoreless innings in the Reds' surprising World Series sweep of the Oakland A's.

The Unintimidator

Tug McGraw did it differently from such flame-throwing relievers as Goose Gossage, Rob Dibble, and Billy Wagner. He had no fastball, relying instead on a befuddling screwball. He didn't glower; he grinned. His spirit, competitiveness, and pitching smarts carried him through a nineteen-year career that included seven postseason visits and two World Championships—during which he never lost his irrepressible, often downright goofy, personality. "I have no trouble with the twelve inches between my elbow and my palm," he said. "It's the seven inches between my ears that's bent."

The Mad Hungarian

In the mid-1970s, when he was an intense reliever for the St. Louis Cardinals, no one in baseball was more fun to watch than Al Hrabosky. Stalking around the mound, glaring toward home from behind his bushy beard and mustache, muttering imprecations, and pounding a cloud of dust from the rosin bag, he looked like he wanted nothing more than to unleash a fastball at the batter's head. His act was very effective: In 1975 he posted a 1.66 ERA and a league-leading 22 saves in 97 innings. "When I'm on the road," he once said proudly, "my greatest ambition is to get a standing boo."

Take a Seat, Buddy!

Umpire John Shulock leaves no doubt as to whether a pitch was over the plate or not. He's also preparing to present his back to the batter, in case an argument ensues—which it does often enough in the life of the ump. As the great pitcher Christy Mathewson once said, "Many baseball fans look upon an umpire as a sort of necessary evil to the luxury of baseball, like the odor that follows an automobile." And many players feel the same way.

The Hitmaker

In the 1970s some things were as predictable as the dawn. Pete Rose would get his uniform dirty. Reggie Jackson would make headlines. And Bill Madlock would bat over .300. From 1974 to 1978 Madlock exceeded that benchmark five times in a row, peaking at a league-leading .354 in 1976. By the time he wrapped it up in 1987, he'd batted over .300 nine times and led the league on four separate occasions, on his way to a lifetime .305 mark.

Manager at Work

Sometimes you just have to blow off steam. Cleveland Indians manager Pat Corrales makes his views known to the ump. Never seeming entirely comfortable as a manager, the often-irascible Corrales was only 572–634 in eight years of managing the Texas Rangers, Philadelphia Phillies, and Cleveland Indians. But since his last managerial job (in 1987), he has thrived as a bench coach, spending 1999–2006 beside Bobby Cox with the Atlanta Braves before moving to the Washington Nationals for the 2007 season.

Manager in Repose

To anyone who ever watched Billy Martin as a player or manager, this is a remarkable shot: He actually looks relaxed. (Though, as always, he is alert and watchful, looking for any chance to take advantage of the opponent's weakness.) In his prime, Martin seemed always to be in motion, challenging the umpires, his players, even the fans and his team's owners in his relentless desire to win at all costs. "The day I become a good loser, I'm quitting baseball," he said upon being named the Minnesota Twins' manager in 1969. He never became a good loser, and he never quit fighting for his teams.

Dirty but Happy

The Toronto Blue Jays' Lloyd Moseby celebrates a run scored while disgruntled Kansas City Royals commiserate. For several years in the mid-1980s, the Blue Jays boasted perhaps the best outfield of their era: the speedy Moseby (who once hit fifteen triples in a season), George Bell (a superb run producer), and Jesse Barfield (a consistent Gold Glove outfielder who also hit as many as 40 home runs). No wonder Toronto ended each season either at or near the top of the American League East.

First Contact

Even as baseball has reached new heights of popularity in recent years, setting one attendance record after another, it sometimes seems that the distance between individual players and fans has grown into an unbridgeable gulf. But there is still the chance for a connection, a never-to-be-forgotten moment of human contact—and, perhaps, the birth of a new lifetime fan.

Gardening

Except when they're racing a downpour to pull the tarp over the infield, or dancing to "YMCA" in the middle innings, the grounds crew is the least noted cog in the great machine that is a major-league game. Someone's got to tend all those carefully cropped blades of grass, damped-down stretches of infield dirt, and perfectly straight chalk lines.

How Do They Do It?

"Using your arm to throw a baseball ninety-five miles an hour or more," wrote Alan Schwarz and Gina Kolata in the *New York Times*, "has long been considered about as natural an act for a human as flapping them while jumping off a cliff." This frozen image of Rick Aguilera in motion is stark evidence of the remarkable stress placed on a fragile limb... often more than a hundred times a game. No wonder today's hurlers treat their pitching arms as their most precious possessions.

Preparing for Arrival

Watching ballplayers (like Henry Blanco here) in the heat of the game, it's hard to understand why they're not injured all the time. They must be willing to put their bodies at risk at any moment for the good of the team, even at the cost of their career. To prevent this, teams employ an armada of professionals. "We have four doctors, three therapists, and five trainers," Tommy Lasorda marveled while he was managing the Dodgers. "Back when I broke in, we had one trainer, who carried a bottle of rubbing alcohol—and by the seventh inning he'd drunk it all."

The Hammy

Even a cursory search through the injury reports each season shows that probably the most vulnerable spot on the baseball player's body is the hamstring. At any moment, those long muscles running up the back of the thigh can cramp, pull, or even tear, putting a player on the shelf for weeks. Here, a New York Mets trainer does what he can to prevent a hamstring injury. Still, there's a limit to what's possible in a game so filled with twisting and turning and sudden bursts of speed.

Just Another Day at the Office

What Tommy Lasorda once said about Mike Scioscia (here crashing into Gary Carter in 1992, the final year of both their careers) applied equally to almost every catcher. "If he raced his pregnant wife," Lasorda said, "he'd finish third." But who would fault a catcher for lack of foot speed? By the time they were done, for example, Carter and Scioscia had played a total of thirty-two seasons (nearly 3,500 games) crouched behind the plate and absorbing crushing blows from runners barreling into them. It's a marvel that they could even walk.

Staying in Shape

Never the most physically gifted player on the field, Steve Garvey was an exercise fanatic, working as hard as any player in baseball at conditioning. The results were spectacular: Garvey was a kind of mini–Iron Horse, playing 155 or more games 11 times in his career, and the full season—every single game—an astonishing six times in a row between 1975 and 1980. Getting every last ounce out of his ability, he chalked up 200 or more hits in a season six times, on his way to a lifetime total of 2,599.

The Secret to Lasting Forever

Roger Clemens' career began in 1984, and with his return to the Yankees in 2007 he demonstrated once again a resilience shared by only a few pitchers in baseball history. By then, he'd pitched more than 200 innings 15 times; won more than 20 games 6 times; and captured the Cy Young Award 7 times. How did he do it? According to the Rocket himself, he relied on an almost obsessive fitness regimen that covered every day of the season—and of the year. "My only day off is the day I pitch," he once said.

Ice, Ice Baby

One of Roger Clemens' fitness tips is to use ice liberally on the pitching arm. Does this really help prevent injuries? For decades pitchers have thought so, but the scientific proof is lacking. Some experts think it might be better to let the arm recover by keeping it in gentle motion for a while after pitching. Still, who's going to argue with the Rocket, who was still going strong more than two decades after his 1984 debut?

The Bird

It was one of the best stories in baseball's rich history: the arrival of Mark "The Bird" Fidrych, the young pitcher who took baseball by storm in 1977, winning 19 games and making the All-Star team. Marching around the mound, talking to the ball, grinning and joking, he was a breath of fresh air in a game that sometimes seemed to need one. Sadly, just a year later he hurt his arm (it was a torn rotator cuff, though undiagnosed at the time), and was never able to overcome the injury. Here he is in 1979, trying an unsuccessful comeback.

Still Purring

One of the most charismatic, upbeat players of his day, Andres ("The Big Cat") Galarraga was a slugging first baseman who batted .370 one year, hit as many as 47 homers, and drove in 100 or more runs five times. Then, in the spring of 1999, all eyes turned to him when he was diagnosed with non-Hodgkin's lymphoma, a type of cancer. Galarraga missed the entire season while undergoing treatment—but amazingly fought his way back to the bigs in 2000, at the age of 39, to enjoy several more productive years. Here he is in 2001, smiling as usual.

A Delicate Instrument

No one knows exactly why a pitcher's arm goes bad, but there's no question that pitchers who have thrown a huge number of innings in a season tend to get hurt within the next year or two. Case in point: Matt Keough of the Oakland A's, who pitched 250 innings in 1980, including—tellingly—an astonishing 20 complete games. Then his arm began to hurt. He reached 200 innings pitched just once more, and by 1987, when he was just thirty-two, his major-league career was over.

Survivor

A scrappy, hard-nosed player from his debut in 1982, Jim Eisenreich batted .303 in his first year with Minnesota, but it soon became apparent that something was wrong. Eisenreich began to show uncontrollable physical symptoms, first diagnosed as "anxiety attacks," that soon grew so bad that he retired in 1984. After treatment for what turned out to be Tourette's Syndrome, Eisenreich returned with the Kansas City Royals in 1987 and by 1989 had developed into a consistent .300 hitter, reaching .362 for the Philadelphia Phillies in 1996. He ended his career in 1998 with a .280 lifetime average and 1,160 hits—a testament to his skills and determination alike.

He Wouldn't Take No for an Answer

Jim Abbott, a phenomenal athlete with ferocious stuff—and a left-hander to boot—dreamed of being a major leaguer. Abbott's only problem was that he had been born without a right hand. But that didn't stop him. After starring in college and helping the United States win a gold medal in 1988 Olympics, he moved to the California Angels in 1989, winning 12 games his rookie year, and following that up in 1991 with an 18–11 record. "I've learned that it's not the disability that defines you," said Abbott. "It's how you deal with the challenges the disability presents you with."

Look Here, Whippersnapper!

Some managers seem like they've been around since the game began. Sparky Anderson (right) was one of them—and, with that shock of white hair, he also looked like he possessed the wisdom of the ages. His first major-league managing job was with the Cincinnati Reds from 1970 to '78, during which time the Big Red Machine merely won four pennants and two World Series. Moving to the Detroit Tigers in 1980, he presided over another championship in 1984. Here he gives some advice to young gun Lou Piniella, manager of the Seattle Mariners.

Dawn of a New Era

In 1969 each league was split into two divisions and a playoff round was added prior to the World Series. The first year's Championship Series brought together the Atlanta Braves and New York Mets in the National League and the Baltimore Orioles and Minnesota Twins in the A.L. Here, Mets announcer Bob Murphy interviews two eventual Hall of Famers: the Braves' Hank Aaron and hometown boy Tom Seaver before the Miracle Mets swept the Braves and went on to pluck the Orioles in the World Series.

Don't Stand So Close to Me

Jim Palmer won twenty or more games a remarkable eight times between 1970 and 1977 and led the Baltimore Orioles to the postseason eight times during his brilliant career. Yet even during perhaps his greatest year, 1970, when he won 20, pitched 305 innings, tossed 5 shutouts, and brought home a World Series championship, he rarely seemed fully happy or relaxed in public. "It is as if Jim feels that it is a sign of weakness if he breaks the ultra-cool facade and displays emotion," suggested *Sporting News*.

Incomparable

Everyone remembers the great Roberto Clemente for his spectacular performance in the Pirates' 1971 World Series championship, his charitable works, and his tragic early death. What is less well remembered is that Clemente did everything well, year in and year out. "He was the best I ever played with," his teammate Dock Ellis told the writer Phil Pepe. "He did things I never saw done before in baseball. As a hitter, a runner, an outfielder, throwing the ball, running the ball down, going up on the wall, up on the screen, throwing to all four bases."

Rise of the Machine

The Cincinnati Reds celebrate their NLCS sweep over the Pittsburgh Pirates in 1970. Their subsequent appearance in the World Series was the first for team stalwarts Johnny Bench, Tony Perez, and Pete Rose, but it was far from the last. The Reds would return to the postseason in 1972, 1973, 1975, 1976, and 1979 and bring home World Series championships in '75 and '76. "I've said it before, and I'll say it again," said Reds manager Sparky Anderson in 1970. "I think I manage the best team in baseball."

Eye of the Storm

Between 1968, when he took over the team, and 1982 Earl Weaver led the Baltimore Orioles to ninety-plus wins ten times, including four pennants and the 1970 World Series championship. Throughout, he was a brilliant tactician with a stoical, frequently hard-edged disposition—tough on umpires, opponents, even his own team. "You know Earl," said Elrod Hendricks, an Orioles catcher during the glory years. "He's not happy unless he's not happy."

Exactly Where They Wanted To Be

Exuding self-confidence, Oriole stars Paul Blair and Frank Robinson await a World Series game in 1970. Blair, an incomparable fielder, went 9–19 (.474) during the Series, while the thirty-five-year-old Robinson slugged two home runs and drove in four. Add Jim Palmer, Mike Cuellar, and Dave McNally at their peaks and Brooks Robinson playing third better than anyone had ever played it before, and it's no surprise that the Orioles won the Series with ease in five games over the Cincinnati Reds.

Captain Hook

Though he had not yet developed his full reputation as a man in a hurry to go to the bullpen, Reds manager Sparky Anderson was well aware by 1970 that starting pitching was not his team's greatest strength—but that keeping the score close might allow his brilliant offense to come back. Exhibit A in Sparky's defense came in Game Four, when he pulled starter Gary Nolan in the third inning. At the time, the Reds trailed 4–2—and then they came back to win the game, 6–5, for their only victory of the Series.

Now Pinch-Hitting ... Leroy Neiman!

Neiman, the popular artist, seemed to be everywhere during big events of the 1970s, painting everyone from Joe Namath to Muhammed Ali. Here, sporting the trademark curling mustache that would have been more in fashion with the era's hirsute Oakland A's than the clean-shaven Cincinnati Reds, Neiman gets some baseball lessons from a future Hall of Famer, the patient Johnny Bench.

Return of the Bombers

The Yankees had made their first move back into their accustomed position on top of the American League in 1976, grabbing their first pennant since 1964, but then were almost effortlessly swept by the Cincinnati Reds in the World Series. The next year the Yankees' relatively easy six-game victory over Los Angeles in the World Series—featuring Reggie Jackson's epochal three-homer Game Six—proved that the Bombers were back. Here, the Dodgers' Don Sutton pitches against Lou Piniella.

So Close

In one of the most famous pennant races of all time, a roller-coaster ride full of thrills and heartbreak, the Red Sox came up short against the Yankees in the 163rd game of the 1978 season. That agonizing failure kept Carl Yastrzemski (facing camera, with Jim Rice [#14] and Jerry Remy) from one final chance to win a World Series, after a pair of agonizing seven-game disappointments in 1967 and 1975. "The only fault you can find with this club," Yaz said of the '78 team, "is perhaps we all wanted to win too badly."

Tumult

Even before the 1978 Yankees won the pennant and headed into the World Series, every baseball fan on Earth was familiar with the headline-grabbing Bronx Zoo, starring transcendently talkative Reggie Jackson, surly Thurman Munson, irascible Lou Piniella (pictured here) and Graig Nettles, low-key Ron Guidry, and self-confident Goose Gossage, among others. But they sure could play, overcoming a two-game deficit to defeat the Los Angeles Dodgers in six and pocket their second consecutive championship.

Scrap Iron

In almost every World Series there's an unsung player who outshines all but the biggest stars. In 1969 it was the Mets' Al Weis and in 1978, the Yankees' Bucky Dent and Brian Doyle. In 1979, it was the Pirates' Phil Garner's turn to lead his team to a championship. A lifetime .260 hitter but beloved by Bucs fans for his aggressiveness and work ethic, the man nicknamed "Scrap Iron" hit .500 (12–24) in the Series, and his 5 RBI were second on the team to Willie Stargell's 7. Every hit, every RBI was needed as the Pirates came back from a three-games-to-one deficit to win.

Poppy Field

Resplendent in their vivid uniforms of the time, his Pittsburgh Pirate teammates congratulate Willie Stargell on one of the three home runs he slugged during the Bucs' seven-game Series victory over the Orioles in 1979. "Willie Stargell's place in the heart of Baltimoreans is fast approaching that love-and-affection stage shown for a volcano in Pompeii, a flood in Johnstown, and an earthquake in San Francisco," wrote Lowell Reidenbaugh of Pops. "He's pure catastrophe."

We Have Lift-Off

"Sometimes, when I'm nervous, I try to look into the stands to find a friendly face," said Phillies ace Tug McGraw after helping the Phillies clinch a postseason berth in 1980. "I found this guy yawning. I said, 'You'd better not go to sleep. I'm still pitching.'" Nobody, however, was dozing when Tug's brilliant World Series work (a win, two saves, and a 1.17 ERA) helped lead the Phillies to their first-ever championship, a hard-fought six-game victory over George Brett and the Kansas City Royals.

Rare is the World Series whose most brilliant players are both third basemen—especially when both have just completed spectacular seasons that would earn them Most Valuable Player awards. Such was the case, however, in 1980, when Mike Schmidt (48 home runs and 121 RBI during the regular season), pictured here, and George Brett (an astounding .390 batting average) faced off. Today, both men are comfortably ensconced in the Hall of Fame, each having been elected overwhelmingly on the first ballot.

Let's Play Two Hundred

You could tell at one glance that no one enjoyed playing baseball more than George Brett. The infectious pleasure he got from the game was clear from the moment he began his career in 1973 through the day he wrapped it up in 1993. "Some players are great talents. Brett plays to beat you, mercilessly," wrote Peter Gammons in 1980. "If I were to start a team, he is the first player I'd want."

The Perfectionist

He hit only .206 and .196 during his first two shots at the Show, but Mike Schmidt's relentless hard work led to a first-ballot Hall of Fame career that included 548 home runs and 1,595 RBI. In 1980, the first of his three MVP years, Schmidt led the majors in home runs with 48—and the Phillies to their first World Series championship in their 98-year history. "I'm never satisfied," Schmidt once said. "I can't stand satisfaction. To me, greatness comes from that quest for perfection."

Pugnacious

If there was a pennant race nearby in the late 1970s and early 1980s, the Phillies were in it—and Larry Bowa (#10, with Pete Rose on the right) was a big reason why. A fiery player, annoying in the extreme to opposing teams, Bowa was a good-hitting shortstop and gold-glove fielder whose impact on the Phillies transcended the numbers. He was never satisfied with second place, and if he made a lot of noise telling his teammates so, they responded in kind.

Nightmare Scenario

Dave Winfield is out once again during the 1981 World Series, which was a total loss for the New York Yankee star from beginning to end. Winfield could boast just a lone single in 22 at-bats as the Yankees fell to the Dodgers in six messy games. Luckily, the future Hall of Famer got another, more successful chance to win a Series more than a decade later, during the Toronto Blue Jays' 1992 championship season.

Education of a Pitcher

In 1978 the Dodgers' Bob Welch (left, with Davey Lopes and Steve Yeager) was a twenty-one-year-old rookie facing the towering Yankees in the World Series. He ended Game Two by striking out Mr. October himself, Reggie Jackson, with the bases loaded—only to have Reggie blast a home run off him in the decisive Game Six. In 1981, though the Dodgers won the Series, Welch's experience was even worse: He failed to record an out in his Game Four start.

Right Place, Right Time

Don Baylor (sneaking into second base ahead of Chicago White Sox' Don Kessinger's tag) was a solid ballplayer during his 19-year career, hitting more than 20 home runs nine times and ending up with more than 2,100 hits, 300 home runs, and 1,200 RBI. His timing was great, too. He was repeatedly able to join a team just in time to help it make the playoffs: After two postseason trips with the Orioles and two more with the Angels, he ended his career with World Series appearances with the Red Sox (1986), Twins (1987), and A's (1988).

The Goose

Goose Gossage was the star reliever of the great Yankee teams of the late 1970s and early 1980s, playing an important role (six innings pitched, no runs, and one hit allowed) in the team's great 1978 World Series victory. One of the secrets of the Goose's success: He pitched like some out-of-control machine, hurling his big body and the hardball with such velocity that-batters quailed out of the way. "It's a scary feeling, a violent feeling, and I'm not a violent person," he said of his emotions on the mound. "There's not a soft spot in my heart for any hitter."

Just in Time

The 1981 World Series was not a thing of beauty. The Yankees, in the last hurrah for the great team that had won back-to-back championships in 1977–78, were in far from peak form, hitting only .238 over the course of six games. The aging Dodgers weren't at their best, either (Davey Lopes, their second baseman, committed a Series-record six errors). In the end, the pitching of young Fernando Valenzuela and old Burt Hooton, and the hitting of Pedro Guerrero (2 HRs, 7 RBI), was enough to carry L.A. to a six-game victory.

Not Quite Enough

The Milwaukee Brewers' Robin Yount had some year in 1982. During the regular season, he hit .331 with 46 doubles, 12 triples, 29 home runs, and 114 RBI. Then, after a quiet League Championship Series, which the Brewers won over California anyway, he came roaring back in the World Series, going 12–29 with a homer and six runs batted in. "I just want to win a world championship," he said at the time, but, alas, it was not to be, as the Brewers fell to the St. Louis Cardinals in seven games.

Center of the World

The Cardinals are more than a baseball team to St. Louis and much of the rest of the Midwest: They're almost a religion. After a hiatus of nearly fifteen years, the team's return to the World Series in 1982 was cause for regional celebration. Icing on the cake was the Cardinals' exciting seven-game Series victory over the Milwaukee Brewers (who had their own Midwestern fan base), culminating in a hard-fought, 6–3 Game Seven win at pulsating Busch Stadium.

Whatever It Takes

The Brewers' Robin Yount burrows safely into third base underneath the Cardinals' Ken Oberkfell in a typically hard-fought moment in the 1982 Series. Getting down and dirty was the Brewers' defining characteristic in 1982, as they proudly featured such unkempt stars as Gorman Thomas, Mike Caldwell, and Moose Haas. The trim Cardinals, on the other hand, were built for speed and defense. As it turned out, however, the Cardinals both outhit and outpitched the Brew Crew, leading to St. Louis's first championship since 1968.

Only the Best

Ozzie Smith flashes some leather against the Brewers' Robin Yount in the 1982 Series. It's generally accepted that Ozzie was the best-fielding shortstop of all time, but what's less generally remembered is that he worked himself up to being an offensive force as well. After never exceeding .230 in his last three years in San Diego, he hit as high as .295 with the Cardinals, struck thirty or more doubles four times, and stole a total of 580 bases. "When I'm in my groove," he said, "there is no thinking. Everything just happens."

Man Out of Time

Jim Palmer was a symbol of the Baltimore Orioles' success in the 1960s and 1970s, and he hung on into 1983. During the regular season, the future Hall of Famer went just 5–4 in 14 appearances, but benefited when the Orioles, led by Eddie Murray and Cal Ripken, headed to the World Series once again. In the Fall Classic, he pitched two innings in Game Three, just a day before his thirty-eighth birthday—and got the win. It was the last win, regular- or postseason, of Palmer's career.

New Star in Town

By 1983 the old stars of the Baltimore Orioles—Brooks and Frank Robinson, Dave McNally and Jim Palmer—were either long gone or at the end of their careers. The players who carried the team to the Series were future Hall of Famers Eddie Murray (33 HRs, 111 RBI, .306 BA) and Cal Ripken, Jr., who won the MVP with a stunning season that included 211 hits, 47 doubles, 27 HRs, 102 RBI, and a .318 batting average. Though neither Murray nor Ripken (here with Philadelphia's Ivan DeJesus) shone in the Series, it didn't matter: The Orioles won in five games.

Young Mr. October

Reggie Jackson hit his last World Series home run in 1981, so by 1984 the game was waiting for another young star to assume the mantle of World Series hero. Why not the burly, rugged Kirk Gibson, who played baseball as if he'd wandered in from a football game? In the Tigers' five-game utter domination of the overmatched San Diego Padres, Gibson hit .333 with two home runs—including an epochal blast against Goose Gossage that put an exclamation point on Game Five.

Mr. Smooth

Quiet, reserved, never attracting many headlines, Lou Whitaker did what all great second basemen should do: He played hard and smart every game, rarely made an error, and pitched in with the bat, amassing a lifetime total of 2,369 hits and slugging fifteen or more home runs eight times in a 19-year career. Here he is with Tony Gwynn during the 1984 Series, during which he played a typically stellar second base, hit .278, and scored 6 of the Tigers' 23 runs.

Lou's Partner

Uncharacteristically for a baseball player in any generation, Lou Whitaker had just one partner at shortstop for eighteen years: Alan Trammell. The two came up together in 1977, and Trammell retired in 1996 (just one year after Whitaker), having amassed 2,365 hits to his partner's 2,369. "One of the most popular Tigers, a bright, cheerful, and witty presence both in the clubhouse and on the field," as *Sports Illustrated* put it, Trammell—pictured here with the Padres' Steve Garvey—batted .450 in the '84 Series, with 2 home runs and 6 RBI.

That Base Is Mine!

Kirk Gibson pulls in safely to third base as the Padres' Gary Templeton applies the late tag. "He is twenty-seven years old, with a thick neck and enormous shoulders," Roger Angell wrote of Gibson after the Tigers' dominating 1984 Series win, "but when you see him up close—in the middle of a boisterous clubhouse party, say, with his blond hair soaked with champagne, and his pale, darting eyes alight with triumph—your first, startled thought is: Look how young he is! Why, he's just a kid—it's all just beginning for him." Angell was half-right: Gibson's career was plagued by injuries, but one more magnificent pennant race—and an all-time World Series moment—did still lie ahead.

First Shot

In 1984, his first full season with San Diego, Tony Gwynn batted .351 with a league-leading 213 hits and carried the Padres to the World Series. "The only way to pitch to Tony," said Al Leiter, "is to throw the ball down the middle and hope he hits it at someone." Yet for all his regular-season heroics (he led the league in hitting eight times), Gwynn and his Padres never quite achieved the ultimate triumph. In their two Series appearances, 1984 and 1998, they won a total of one game.

What It Takes

Jack Morris, shown here pitching in the 1984 Series, didn't quite accumulate Hall of Fame numbers during his eighteen-year career. (He finished with a 254–186 record and a 3.90 ERA.) But in a big game, there was no one you wanted more than the uncompromising right-hander with the ferocious split-finger fastball. "Deep down I wonder if Babe Ruth could have hit the split-finger," the self-confident Morris once speculated.

The Hitter

"George Brett could roll out of bed on Christmas morning and hit a line drive," said hitting coach Charlie Lau. And then do it again—all the while demonstrating the pure adrenaline rush of playing baseball at the highest possible level. In 1985, after coming close many times, this Hall of Famer led his Kansas City Royals to the World Championship, batting .348 with three homers in the League Championship Series and following that up with a .370 mark in the Series.

The Quis

Every so often, a pitcher shows up who has the whole package: a vivid personality, a unique style, and, of course, great talent. The late Dan Quisenberry, the Kansas City Royals' submarining closer during their glory years of the early- and mid-1980s, was the real deal. Between 1981 and 1985 he saved a total of 179 games with an ERA that never approached 3.00. More importantly, he helped lead the Royals to the postseason three times in that span, culminating in their thrilling seven-game victory over the St. Louis Cardinals in 1985. "Like any real good pitcher," acknowledged Earl Weaver, "he messes with the batters' heads."

Sweet Stroke

He was never a true slugger (his season high for home runs was thirty). He had only average speed. He was rarely the biggest, strongest, or most intimidating figure on the field. But George Brett was a *hitter*. Day after day, he unleashed his powerful, unfussy, efficient swing, and day after day he got his hits—3,154 of them before he hung up his spikes in 1993—while seeming happier to be on the field than anyone else. "I play best when I enjoy myself," he once said, something that was perfectly clear to anyone who ever watched him play.

Moment of Truth

Cesar Cedeno had been as responsible as anyone for the St. Louis Cardinals holding off the New York Mets and capturing the National League East in 1985, batting an astonishing .434 with 6 home runs and 19 RBI in 76 late-season at-bats after coming over from the Cincinnati Reds. But his magic, and the Cards', ran out in the World Series. Cedeno hit just .133 and his team fell to Jim Sundberg and the Royals in seven games.

Duck!

The Royals' Willie Wilson had better get out of the way, because the Cardinals' Ozzie Smith owns the airspace in this play from the 1985 World Series. Still, Wilson had the last laugh: He batted .367, with 3 stolen bases for the Series, while Smith (who'd hit .276 during the regular season) managed just 2 hits in 23 at-bats. Most importantly of all, the Royals came back from a 3-games-to-2 deficit to capture the Series.

Stone Wall

In the 1980s, Gary Carter was known more for his booming home runs and his ever-present smile than for his defense. The fact is, though, that he was also a three-time Gold Glover, calling a good game, throwing well, and never backing down on plays at the plate. Here, in the 1986 World Series between the New York Mets and Boston Red Sox, he prepares for the arrival of Sox behemoth Jim Rice.

The Gnat

In 1986, his first full year with the Mets, Lenny Dykstra was just a 23-year-old, 5'10", 160-pound flyweight in the land of giant sluggers. But he put all his talents to use through constant effort and intense focus on the game, hitting .295 for the season, with 27 doubles, 7 triples, 8 home runs, and 31 stolen bases in just 431 at-bats. He then went on to hit .296 in the World Series, with 2 home runs—including the leadoff shot against Oil Can Boyd in Game Three that started the Mets on their famous comeback from two games down.

Stunned Belief!

To the joy and astonishment of his teammates, Ray Knight scores the winning run in the bottom of the tenth inning of Game Six of the 1986 Series. Down two runs to the Red Sox with two outs and nobody on, the Mets strung together three singles, a wild pitch, and one eternally infamous error by Bill Buckner to complete perhaps the most astonishing comeback in Series history. "It's baseball," said the Sox' Dave Henderson after his team's heartbreaking loss. "It's baseball, and we've got to live with it."

The Pinnacle

Two days after the stunning conclusion of Game Six, the Mets and Red Sox played the ultimate game of the 1986 Series. Though Boston jumped out to a 3–0 lead, no one could have been surprised when the inexorable Mets rampaged through the Sox' shell-shocked bullpen for an 8–5 win and the championship. Here, Tim Teufel, Gary Carter, Wally Backman, and the rest of the team celebrate the Mets' first championship since 1969.

Wait Your Turn, Wade

During the 1986 season Wade Boggs hit .357 (amazingly, his *lowest* batting average between 1985 and 1988) with 47 doubles, a .455 on-base percentage, and 107 runs scored. Like many of his Red Sox teammates, however, Boggs saw his mojo fade in the World Series, when he hit .290 but scored only 3 runs. The future Hall of Famer would have to wait a decade to get his World Series championship—and switch to the Sox' hated American League East rivals, the Bronx Bombers, to do so.

Three Moves Ahead

The St. Louis Cardinals' brilliant manager, Whitey Herzog, addresses a crisis in the 1987 World Series against the Minnesota Twins. "Under Herzog's platinum thatch throbs a brain so alive with stratagems that it might as well belong to a football coach," said *Sports Illustrated*. But for all his acknowledged brilliance, Whitey couldn't prevent his Cardinals from falling to Kirby Puckett and the Twins in seven games.

Two of a Kind

When you're at the pinnacle of your profession, you're allowed to act like every moment of every game isn't an act of open war—even during the World Series. Here the Cardinals' Ozzie Smith and the Twins' Kirby Puckett share a laugh during the '87 Series, which served to introduce Kirby to the world. On the big stage for the first time, Puckett didn't disappoint, batting .357, playing the outfield with élan, and helping lead the Twins to a surprising seven-game victory over the favored Cardinals.

The Reward

It's just a ring—and, some would argue, not even the most beautiful one ever crafted. But to any baseball player, it represents the holy grail, the pinnacle of achievement, the highest reward for all the hard work that goes into a baseball career. In the 1987 World Series, Twins pitcher Frank Viola won two games, including the deciding seventh game, and received this piece of jewelry to commemorate his achievement.

"Unbelievable!"

The 1988 World Series between the Los Angeles Dodgers and Oakland A's was as much of a David and Goliath story as can be imagined. The A's, led by Bash Brothers Jose Canseco and Mark McGwire, were considered overwhelming favorites. That is, until Kirk Gibson, whose injured legs were supposed to keep him out entirely, hobbled to the plate in the bottom of the ninth against the A's dominating Dennis Eckersley... and slammed this game-winning home run.

In Trouble? No Way!

Los Angeles Dodgers pitching coach Ron Perranoski and second baseman Steve Sax consult with Orel Hershiser during Game Five of the 1988 World Series against the Oakland A's. The picture does not tell the whole story: Hershiser had the reeling A's under his thumb throughout the Series, shutting them out 6–0 in Game Two and then clinching the Series for the upstart Dodgers with an easy 5–2 win in Game Five. "I just have a complete desire to learn and to work hard," Orel said, to the A's dismay.

Lights Out

Orel Hershiser looked unassuming, but on the mound he was a bulldog. A fine, but not outstanding, pitcher since his first full year in 1984, he blossomed into something much more in 1988—and had one of the greatest years in pitching history. He went 23–8 during the regular season, finishing the year with a record-setting 59 consecutive scoreless innings. He then pitched beautifully in the playoffs against the heavily favored Mets before leading the Dodgers to a surprisingly easy Series win over the powerful A's.

Enjoy It While You Can

The A's Mark McGwire enjoys his game-winning ninth inning home run in Game Three of the 1988 World Series. But it was the A's only moment to cheer in the entire Series—Dodger pitching held McGwire and fellow slugger Jose Canseco to an astonishing two hits in thirty-six at-bats. The rest of the team didn't do much better, as the A's batted just .177 as a team during the five-game loss.

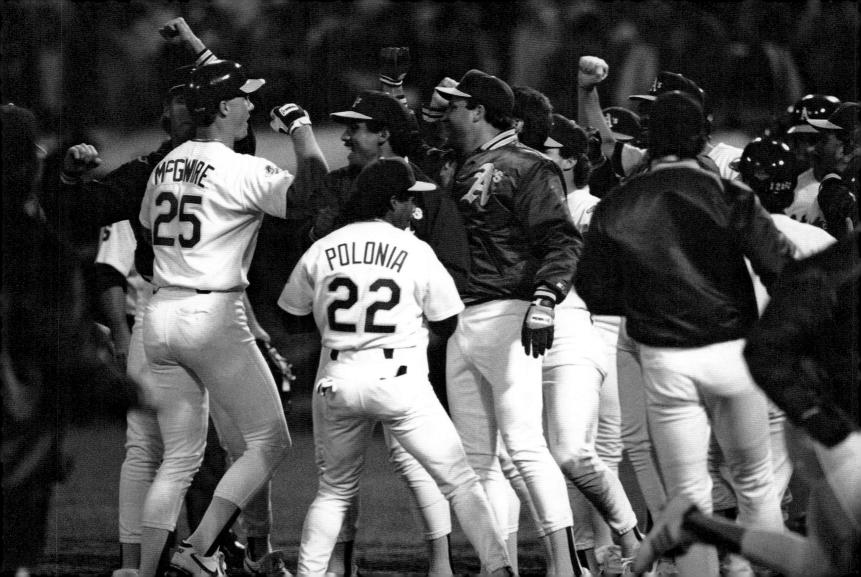

Almost Perfect

It may have been the best year any closer has ever had. During the 1989 regular season, Dennis Eckersley (facing camera) posted a 1.56 ERA and 33 saves as his Oakland A's cruised in the A.L. West. He was just as good in the ALCS against the Toronto Blue Jays, saving three games, and in the World Series against the San Francisco Giants, giving up no hits in two appearances. Said Eckersley, who'd spent the first thirteen years of his career as a starter, "When I started finishing games and coming off the field shaking hands, it was a beautiful thing. I mean, you start seeing that you're an important part of the team." And how!

One-Man Army

Rickey Henderson, in total control during the 1989 World Series. Henderson had a spectacular Series, batting .474 with a double, two triples, a home run, and three stolen bases in the four games. Still, it was the havoc he created on the bases that may have been his most powerful weapon. "If you walk him," an anonymous opposing-team scout told *Sports Illustrated* during the Series, "you might as well build a freeway from home plate, over the mound, and right to second base."

Baseball Came Second

The 1989 Fall Classic was put into perspective by the violent earthquake (6.9 on the Richter scale) that struck the Bay Area on October 17, just minutes before Game Three was set to begin. "I didn't really feel the quake at first," said Bob Welch (center, leaving the field with his wife, Mary Ellen), who was under the stands preparing to start the game. "I thought they were rolling barrels on the ramps above the clubhouse." But he, and everyone else at Candlestick, soon learned the devastating truth.

Hero

Pitcher Dave Stewart was nearly perfect in the 1989 postseason, going 2–0 in both the playoffs and the World Series. His on-the-field achievements, however, were overshadowed by his work in the community after the powerful earthquake shook the Bay Area mid-Series. Stewart, who was born in Oakland, was a visible presence in the city during the nearly two-week delay before the Series resumed, helping start both the healing and the rebuilding process. "We will endure," he said. "We will rebuild."

Authority

Cincinnati Reds stars Paul O'Neill, Barry Larkin, Chris Sabo, and Eric Davis listen intently to Manager Lou Piniella's message prior to a 1990 World Series game. "I didn't come here to manage—I came here to win," Piniella said upon being named Reds manager before the season. His young team, featuring few players with any playoff experience at all, responded to this uncompromising attitude by making one of the most surprising races to the Series of any team in years.

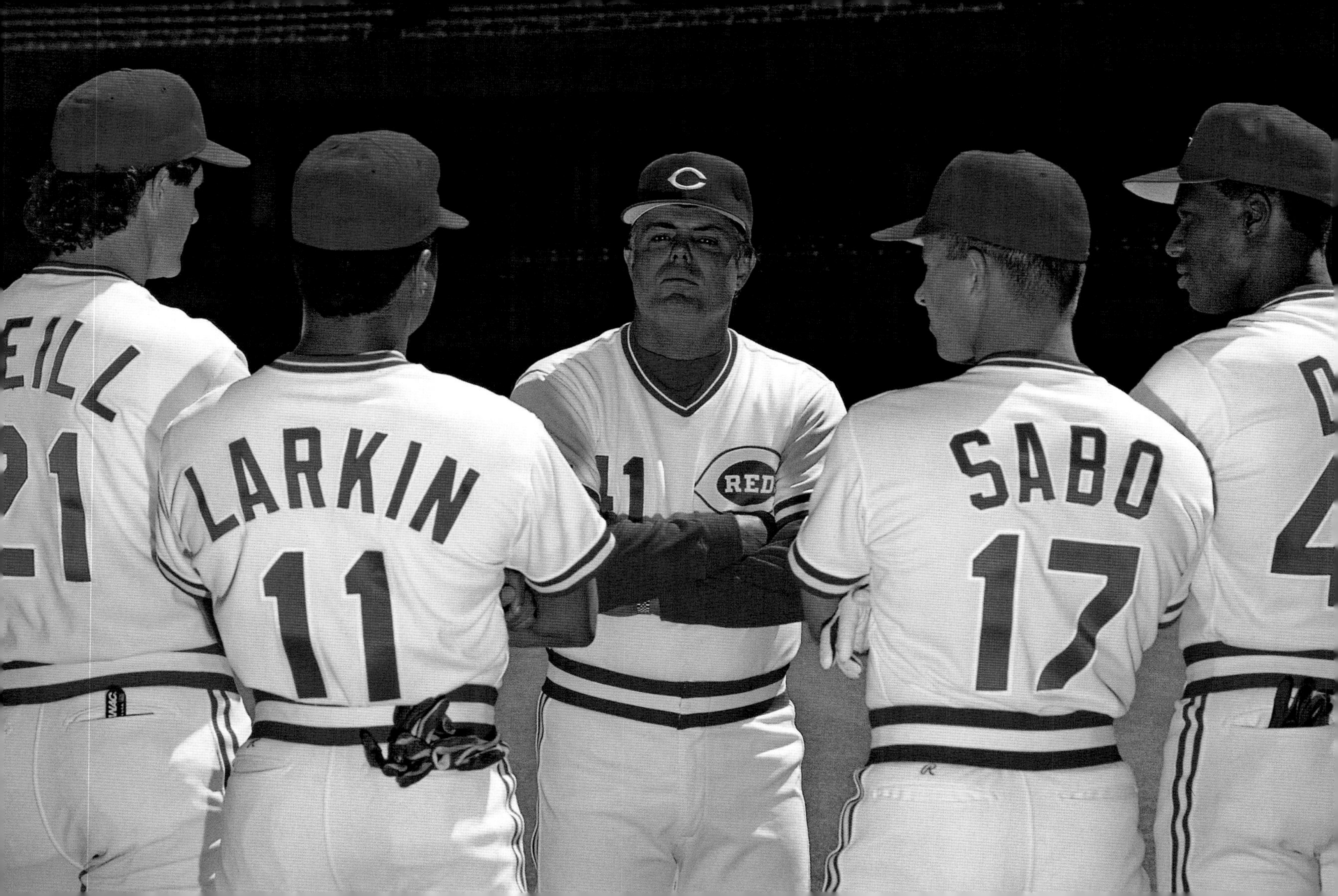
EILL
21
LARKIN
11
RED
SABO
17

Pinch Me

Cincinnati's Barry Larkin and Mariano Duncan celebrate their remarkable Series sweep of the heavily favored Oakland A's in the 1990 World Series. The inexperienced Reds' domination over the A's was almost total: They mustered a .317 Series batting average versus .207 for the A's, scoring 22 runs compared to just 8. Outfielder Billy Hatcher hit .750 and third baseman Chris Sabo .563 for the Reds, compared to .083 for Jose Canseco and .214 for Mark McGwire. It was a mismatch from start to finish.

Not With a Bang

The Oakland A's Carney Lansford managed to hit .267 in the 1990 World Series, garnering 4 singles in 15 at-bats but failing to drive in or score a run. Still, his accomplishments far overshadowed those of most of his teammates: The A's hit just .207 as a team against the underdog Cincinnati Reds, scoring a total of 8 runs as they lost the Series in 4 games. In a classic of understatement, Tom Barnidge wrote in *Sporting News*, "It was not exactly the kind of performance from which legends are born."

Wow, That Was Quick

The scores were 7–0, 5–4, 8–3, 2–1, and the winning team was the same in every game: The Cincinnati Reds were among the most unexpected World Champions of all time. Led by only one certified star (shortstop Barry Larkin), the team was made up mostly of hardworking role-players like catcher Joe Oliver (facing camera), third-baseman Chris Sabo (in goggles to left), outfielder Paul O'Neill, and a gaggle of strong but not dominant pitchers such as Jose Rijo and Tom Browning. In 1990, it was enough.

Chuck on the Go

After three World Series in which the losing teams totaled a single win, fans deserved a true barn burner. They got one in the 1991 tilt between the Minnesota Twins and the Atlanta Braves, two teams who had finished last in their divisions just a year earlier. But their clash in the Series featured everything from brilliant pitching to great defense to timely hitting—and the Twins' Chuck Knoblauch was at the middle of a lot of it, getting on base twelve times and stealing four bases in the seven games.

Unhittable

He'd had a good year in 1991 (18–12, with a 3.43 ERA) and won two games in the ALCS, but in the postseason the Twins' Jack Morris was something else again. Starting three times in the seven-game Series, he pitched twenty-three innings and gave up only three runs. His crowning achievement was in Game Seven, when he pitched ten shutout innings in the Twins' Series-clinching 1–0 victory. When someone asked him afterward how much longer he could have gone, Morris smiled and said "A hundred and twelve innings."

Rally Caps

John Smoltz (center) and his Braves teammates root on their team in this high-stress moment from the ever-tense 1991 Series. The twenty-three-year-old Smoltz did his part, starting two games and allowing only two earned runs. But it wasn't enough, and though Smoltz pitched magnificently in Game Seven—seven shutout innings—the Twins' Jack Morris was even better, denying Atlanta a well-deserved title.

That Kind of Series

Sometimes it seemed like every moment, every play in the 1991 Series was tense—hard-fought yet clean. As *Sporting News* columnist Dave Kindred described this Game Three play: "Dan Gladden of Minnesota, spikes Ty Cobb high, knocked over Greg Olson. The catcher was seen standing on his left ear, an exclamation point turned upside down. Did Olson straighten up with his fists balled, looking for a fight? No, he simply rose and handed Gladden his cap. This is the show. It's hardball up here."

The North American Pastime

Toronto—and a lot of Canada—celebrated in October 1992 as a World Series game was played outside the confines of the United States for the first time. And that wasn't enough: In a hard-fought Series, the Blue Jays—led by veterans Jimmy Key, Joe Carter, and Dave Winfield—held off the tough Atlanta Braves to win Canada's first World Championship as well.

Igniters

The speedy Otis Nixon of the Braves was a thorn in the side of the Blue Jays all throughout the 1992 Series, hitting .297, stealing five bases in the six games, and playing stellar outfield defense. He also, however, made the final out of the Series on an attempted bunt base hit with the tying run on third in the bottom of the eleventh inning of Game Six. On the other hand, Blue Jays superstar Roberto Alomar batted only .208 in the Series, with no RBI—but walked away with his first championship ring.

Where the Championships Were

Paul Molitor played the first fifteen years of his career with the Milwaukee Brewers, and the closest he ever came to a championship was a disappointing loss to the St. Louis Cardinals in 1982. Before the 1993 season Molitor chose to sign with the defending-champion Blue Jays—and with his help (211 hits and a .332 batting average during the regular season), the team got back to the Series again. And, boy, did Molitor contribute: He batted .500, with 2 doubles, 2 triples, 2 home runs, and 8 RBI, as the Jays defeated the Phillies in 6 games.

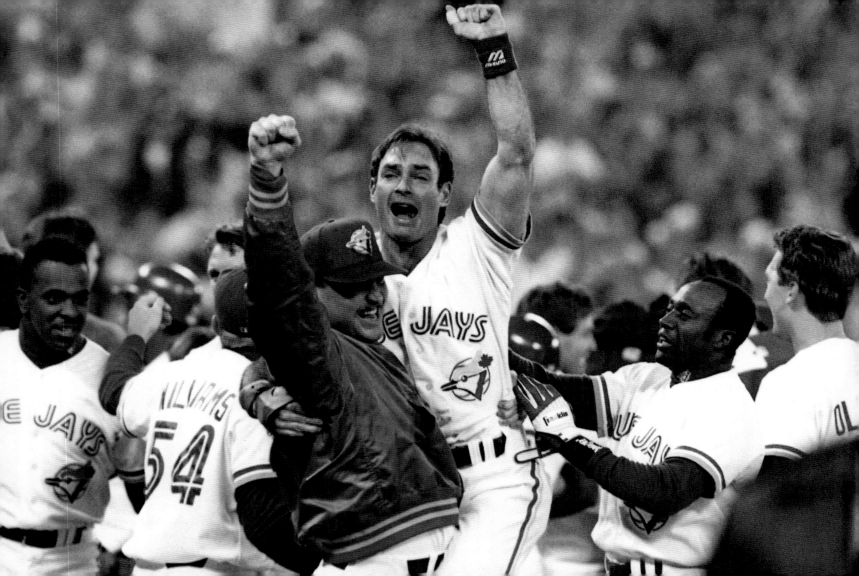

He Could Do It All

At his best, Roberto Alomar (shown here during the 1993 World Series) was one of the greatest second basemen of all time, as Orlando Cepeda attested: "I saw Cool Papa Bell play," Cepeda recalled. "I played with Julian Javier, Felix Millan, and Cookie Rojas. I played against Bill Mazeroski and Joe Morgan. In All-Star Games, I saw Rod Carew. As good as they were, none of them were as good as Roberto Alomar."

Stealing Home?

Workers at the Toronto SkyDome dig up the field after Game Two of the 1993 World Series. With the Series tied at a game apiece, the Blue Jays and the Phillies headed off to Philadelphia for the next three games—while the SkyDome switched helmets and prepared to host the Toronto Argonauts of the Canadian Football League. Less than a week later, the plate was back in place, ready for Joe Carter's three-run home run that would give Toronto its second straight Series championship.

Don't Forget, Cito!

Even at the height of the most important, most intense few days of the baseball season—the World Series—teams have responsibilities to the fans and the business of baseball that extend beyond the games themselves. Before Game Two of the 1993 Series between Toronto and Philadelphia, the Blue Jays' clubhouse contained rows of boxes of balls, each one marked with instructions (actually more like commands) to the players, the coaches, and even Manager Cito Gaston. No mention is made of who the lucky recipients of the signed balls might be.

Rawlings
Baseballs
Coach, and CITO,
PLEASE sign one ball each
on the sweet spot!

Pucker Up

Rickey Henderson delivers a smooch to the World Series trophy while a delighted Joe Carter looks on after the Blue Jays' six-game defeat of the Phillies in the 1993 Series. Both men were involved in the crucial last of the ninth inning of Game Six: Henderson took a walk from Phillies' closer Mitch Williams, and—after an out and a single—Carter delivered the three-run home run that won the game and the Series. "I'm kind of a private person," Carter said afterward. "All this might change that now… but I'll gladly suffer the consequences."

Sea of Green

Atlanta Braves pitchers Steve Avery and Kent Mercker await a game in the 1995 World Series against the Cleveland Indians. In 1995, with the splitting of each league into three divisions and the addition of an extra round of playoffs, it became harder than ever to make it to the Series. But the Braves, led by Avery and ace starters Greg Maddux, Tom Glavine, and John Smoltz, stormed through the Colorado Rockies and Cincinnati Reds to make their third appearance in the past four Series.

Cool As Ice

At his peak, there was probably no pitcher in the National League who drove batters crazier than Tom Glavine. He never threw especially hard, but his masterful control allowed him to place the ball exactly where he wanted, leading (some batters complained) to his getting strike calls even on balls out of the strike zone. His magic continued against the Indians in the 1995 World Series, when he posted two wins and a 1.29 ERA—including a one-hit shutout in the deciding Game Six as the Braves captured their first Series since 1957.

In the Beginning

Derek Jeter celebrates the Yankees' 1996 American League Division Series (ALDS) victory over the Texas Rangers. It was Jeter's rookie year (he'd hit .314), and he was already proving himself a master of the big moment: In the ALDS, he hit .412. "I'm telling you, this kid might be a rookie in name," said Yankee coach Willie Randolph, a former All-Star infielder himself, "but in mind, heart and ability, he's got to be a six-year veteran, because that's exactly how he plays."

Today's Lineup

Jermaine Dye, Fred McGriff, and coach Pat Corrales at the 1996 World Series. It's hard to remember now, so many Yankee championships later, but the Braves were the heavy favorites going into the Series. After all, they were the defending champions, while the Yankees hadn't sniffed the postseason since 1981. The Braves even won the first two games before it All-Started going sour for them... and a new Yankee dynasty was born.

Unexpected Hero

Behind two games to one to the favored Braves, the Yankees were trailing, 6–3, in Game Four when Jim Leyritz came to the plate with two men on in the eighth inning to face the fireballer Mark Wohlers. Wohlers threw a 100-mph fastball, which Leyritz fouled straight back. "You could see a look on Wohlers's face," recalled Yankee pitcher David Cone. "He'd given him his best shot, and Jimmy was right on it." So Wohlers threw a slider instead, which Leyritz blasted out of the park. The Bombers went on to win the game and the World Series, their first of four in five years.

Ten Years On

In 1986 Wade Boggs of the Boston Red Sox was on the field when the Sox came within one strike of bringing home a World Series championship—but fell agonizingly short. It was 1996 before the Hall of Fame third baseman was able to claim his first ring, as a thirty-eight-year-old part-time player for the Yankees. It was the only championship of Boggs' seventeen-year career.

All-American Series

Latin America as well as the United States, that is. The Florida Marlins' Edgar Renteria (with Gary Sheffield, right) celebrates his 1997 Series-winning hit in the bottom of the eleventh inning of Game Six against the Cleveland Indians…but Renteria (born in Colombia) was just one of several Latino players to star for each team. Livan Hernandez (Cuba), Sandy Alomar, Jr. (Puerto Rico), Omar Vizquel (Venezuela), and many others helped set the tone for a Series that made major inroads in areas where soccer had long been the number-one sport.

Sailing Away

In keeping with their boat-happy Miami home, the Marlins staged the first-ever World Series celebration water parade. But the joy of victory was tempered by the knowledge that many of the players would not be returning to the small-market Marlins—and, in fact, by 1998 most of the team's stars, including Gary Sheffield, Al Leiter, Moises Alou, and Kevin Brown, had moved on.

Impregnable

The Yankees celebrate their absolutely dominating sweep over the undermanned San Diego Padres in the 1998 World Series. "You watch those guys long enough and you begin to wonder: What's the formula?" asked Padres superstar Tony Gwynn after the Series was over. "What is it you have to do to beat them?" No one figured out an answer to that question till 2001, three Series later, when the Yankees finally lost one.

Intensity

He was never the most famous player on the field, but he may have been the hardest working—and the toughest on himself. Paul O'Neill was a consistent .300 hitter with power during his tenure with the Yankees, but he seemed to take every at-bat, and every failure, as a personal affront—even when the team was steamrolling the opposition, as the Yankees did to the Atlanta Braves in the 1999 World Series. "You play the game to win the game, and not to worry about what's on the back of the baseball card at the end of the year," O'Neill said.

Fan Favorite

Always giving full effort, Bernie Williams quickly won a place in the heart of Yankee fans when he came up as a raw rookie in 1991. It took years for him to establish himself as a star, but became one of the leaders of the team that made the postseason every year between 1995 and 206, his last year. (This photo is from 1999, when the Yanks swept the World Series from the Braves.) Always one of the most popular Bombers, he rewarded the team and the fans with eight .300 seasons, 287 home runs, and four World Championships.

Some Were Luckier than Others

In 2000, for the first time ever, the Yankees and the Mets faced each other in a World Series. It was a flashback to the Subway Series of the 1940s and 1950s, when it seemed like the New York Giants and the Brooklyn Dodgers took turns facing the Yankees every October. Unfortunately for Mets fans, the results didn't differ much from those of half a century earlier: The DiMaggio- and Mantle-led Bombers usually won, and so did the 2000 Jeter-and-Mariano edition, in five games.

THE LUCKIEST FANS
ON THE FACE
OF THE EARTH

Not This Year

A downcast Mike Piazza sees what the future will hold in the 2000 Series. Piazza, the Mets' unquestionable star, did his part in the Series, slamming two home runs, but he couldn't stop the inexorable Yankee machine from steamrolling his team. Every game was close—the largest margin of victory was two runs—but somehow the ultimate outcome never seemed to be in doubt.

Remembering

For Mariano Rivera—and all the other Yankees and Arizona Diamondbacks—the 2001 World Series was shadowed by the horrifying, tragic events of September 11. The two teams wore baseball caps to honor the losses of both the New York Fire Department and New York Police Department—and went out and delivered one of the most exciting, unpredictable World Series of all time to grateful fans.

"We're Back"

Fans at Yankee Stadium let the world know that nothing would keep them from the ballpark during Game Four of the Series. "In an October, even this October, or maybe especially this October, few things speak more clearly of our national character than a plain, simple, glorious baseball game," wrote Dave Kindred in *Sporting News*.

Unbearable Tension

Everyone watching Game Seven of the 2001 Series had at least an inkling of what the Diamondbacks' Curt Schilling was feeling. It had been a remarkable World Series with extraordinary performances on both sides (not the least from Schilling, who'd started three games and pitched brilliantly all three times), but it had all come down to this: the Diamondbacks down by a run and facing the best reliever ever, Mariano Rivera, in the bottom of the ninth.

Was It for Real?

Moments after Luis Gonzalez (facing camera) hit the bloop single that won Game Seven and the World Series for the Diamondbacks, he, Craig Counsell, Curt Schilling, and David Dellucci celebrate on the field. It was the first loss for Mariano Rivera in fifty-two postseason appearances. "They beat me," Rivera said. "They can say they beat me." A fan's sign at Bank One Ballpark (now Chase Field) put it even more simply: "Yankees = History, Diamondbacks = Future."

Enough to Go Around

Who else? Randy Johnson and Curt Schilling share the 2001 Series MVP trophy. Schilling started three games, pitching 21.1 innings with a 1.69 ERA. Johnson started twice and won both times, then relieved Schilling and got the win in the pivotal Game Seven—a day after pitching seven innings. "Focus," Schilling said of his secret, and he could have been speaking for Johnson as well. "Just being focused on the task at hand. It's one inning, one out, one pitch at a time."

His Moment to Shine

Prior to 2002 Barry Bonds had been considered a disappointing postseason player, hitting just one home run in 97 at-bats in twenty-seven division- and championship-series games. All that changed, however, as the slugger rampaged through the 2002 postseason, launching eight home runs, including four in the World Series. Unfortunately for Barry and his San Francisco Giants, it wasn't enough to capture the championship.

Yeah!

The Anaheim Angels' Tim Salmon celebrates his second home run of the 2002 World Series Game Two, an eighth-inning two-run blast that gave the Angels a lead they wouldn't relinquish. It was a game in which the Angels jumped out to leads of 5−0 and 7−4, fell behind 9−7, and then clawed their way to an 11−10 victory. Eleven pitchers gave it a try, the Giants slammed four homers of their own, and the game clocked in at just under four hours in length. But the fans in Anaheim ate up every moment.

Decisive

A dugout full of Angels—and tens of thousands of hometown fans—congratulate Darin Erstad and David Eckstein, who have just scored on a double by Garret Anderson in the third inning of Game Seven in 2002. The Angels plated three runs in the inning to take a 4–1 lead . . . and, despite this being an offensive-minded Series, the final six innings of the game were scoreless. The Giants had come so close to winning their first championship since moving to San Francisco in 1958, but had come up short, while the comparative newcomer Angels (they arrived in 1961) won their first crown.

Uppercut

Like many young sluggers, the Florida Marlins' Miguel Cabrera started out as a true feast-or-famine hitter, slugging home runs and striking out in prodigious numbers. The same trends were in evidence during Cabrera's first appearance in the postseason, in 2003, when he batted .333 with four homers against the Cubs in the NLCS, but followed it up with a .167 performance against the Yankees in the World Series. Still, Cabrera and his Marlins took home the crown.

The Sure Thing

Ever since he was drafted by the Florida Marlins with the second pick of the 1999 draft, people have been predicting great things for Josh Beckett. He possessed ferocious stuff, great control, and a head that seemed screwed on right. In the 2003 postseason, when he was just twenty-three, Beckett made six appearances, pitching as well as any veteran. In Game Six of the World Series, against the titanically favored Yankees, Beckett pitched a complete-game, five-hit shutout to give the Marlins a most unlikely World Championship.

Big Papi

During all the heartbreaking close calls that afflicted the Boston Red Sox during their decades without a World Series title, what the team most often seemed to lack was a true leader. In 2004 they got one: David Ortiz, a player capable of taking a team on his back and carrying it. In the Sox' amazing comeback from three games down to the Yankees in the ALCS, Big Papi hit three homers and drove in eleven runs—including two walk-off game-winning homers. "He's bulletproof, as far as I'm concerned," said Yankee skipper Joe Torre.

The Curse Reversed

The Red Sox players were jubilant, but they couldn't have been as stunned as longtime fans of the team. After more than eighty years, it must have seemed that the Curse of the Bambino would never be brought to an end. But then, in little more than a week, the Sox took four in a row from the Yankees and then went on to sweep the St. Louis Cardinals and deliver to Beantown—to all of New England—its first Series title since 1918. Boston star Manny Ramirez had the best perspective: "I don't believe in curses," he said.

Jose!

Highly touted upon his signing by the Yankees out of Cuba in 2003, Jose Contreras was considered a disappointment during his short stint with the Bombers. Moving on to the White Sox, though, the mercurial Contreras blossomed, winning fifteen games in 2005 and pitching superbly during the White Sox' unexpected postseason run past the Red Sox and Angels and into the World Series. There, he threw seven strong innings against the Astros in Game One, capturing the first of what would turn out to be a four-game sweep.

Their Kind of Town

Chicago's Cellular Field during Game One of the 2005 World Series. The White Sox came into the Series against the Houston Astros as a comparatively little-known team with few big-name stars. That didn't matter, though, as the Sox won the first two games at home, then moved on to Houston, won a fourteen-inning thriller in Game Three, and then took tense Game Four, 1–0. It was the second consecutive World Series sweep and the White Sox' first championship since 1959.

MVP

In a team of talented but low-profile players, Jermaine Dye was the closest thing to a signature star on the White Sox in 2005—a consistent run producer if only an occasional All-Star. But he got hot in the World Series, going 7 for 16 (.438) against the Astros and hitting the homer in the first inning that scored the opening run of the Series. At the end of the Sox' sweep, Dye was awarded the Series Most Valuable Player award.

The Man Least Likely

"You keep seeing names getting marked off and marked off the lineup card," said White Sox utility man Geoff Blum, "and eventually it gets down to the last guy on the totem pole." In the 2005 Series he was that last guy. The result: In his only at-bat of the Series, Blum blasted a homer in the fourteenth inning of Game Three, giving the Sox the victory. The next day, they held on to a 1–0 lead to finish off the brief Series.

Slamming the Door

In 2005 Adam Wainwright pitched a total of two innings for the St. Louis Cardinals, giving up three runs. Then in 2006 he blossomed, becoming one of the league's most reliable relievers. But no one could have predicted his dominance in the postseason: Against the Padres, the Mets, and finally in the World Series against the Detroit Tigers, Wainwright was nearly perfect, allowing no runs in his nine innings of work and garnering five saves.

No Stopping Them

The 2006 Cardinals were one of the most unlikely World Series teams in years. They'd ended the regular season with just eighty-three wins—one of the lowest totals ever—and had somehow managed to overcome both the Padres and the Mets in the playoffs. Still, they seemed to have little chance against the heavily favored Tigers. As it turned out, though, Scott Rolen (approaching second as Placido Polanco awaits the throw in Game Four) and the rest of the Cardinals absolutely dominated a Series that went only five games.

Inevitable

He was never the flashiest All-Star around, or the burliest slugger, or the most blinding speedster. But every season from 1978 to 1998 Paul Molitor went out, played virtually every game, collected his hits (more than 200 four times) and helped his team win. Here Molitor's Minnesota Twins teammates celebrate his career 3,000th hit on September 16, 1996—a milestone that every baseball fan had long known was coming.

Whatever Works

During his major-league career, Wade Boggs was (like many players) a devoted follower of pregame rituals. For example, he always ended infield practice by stepping on the third-, second-, and first-base bags, in order. Most famously, Boggs ate chicken before every game—2,439 chicken dinners in the majors alone. Who knows whether the rituals helped, but something surely enabled Boggs to slam 3,010 hits, including number 3,000 (on August 7, 1999), shown here.

4,192

He lacked the extraordinary physical talents of Roberto Clemente, Willie Mays, Hank Aaron, and other superstars he played against, but no one ever got more out of his ability than Pete Rose. His boundless determination and short, efficient swing allowed him to collect a record 4,256 base hits, including this Number 4,192 (which allowed him to pass Ty Cobb's decades-old mark) on September 11, 1985.

No Chance?

The New York Mets' trade of Nolan Ryan to the California Angels for over-the-hill third baseman Jim Fregosi is rightly touted as one of the worst swaps of all time. But perhaps it never would have worked in New York for Ryan, who always admitted that he couldn't tolerate big-city life. "I was overwhelmed by being there, and truly intimidated," he said. Set free in California, he immediately became the most feared strikeout pitcher of his time—and perhaps of any time.

No One Like Him

Nolan Ryan threw heat for twenty-seven years in the majors, during which he compiled a record-shattering total of 5,714 strikeouts. Here, in 1990, he, Manager Bobby Valentine, and the Texas Rangers celebrate the 300th of Ryan's eventual 324 victories. "Every hitter likes fastballs, just like everybody likes ice cream," said Reggie Jackson, who struck out twenty-two times against Ryan. "But you don't like it when someone's stuffing it into you by the gallon. That's what it feels like when Nolan Ryan's throwing balls by you."

The Beginning

"Early in my career," Cal Ripken, Jr., said, "I decided I never wanted to get out of shape." Armed with this deceptively mild-mannered philosophy, Ripken began a career of almost unprecedented intensity in 1982. His efforts culminated in not only 3,000 hits, but of course the record for playing the most consecutive games in baseball history (2,632). The reward for staying in shape: first-ballot admission to the Hall of Fame in 2007.

Hero of Charm City

Baltimore fans show Cal Ripken, Jr., what they think of him in 1997, fifteen years into his stellar run with the Orioles. "So many good things have happened to me in the game of baseball," the grateful Ripken said. "When I do allow myself a chance to think about it, it's almost like a storybook career. You feel so blessed to have been able to compete this long."

Perfection

It's hard to know what's more remarkable—that the Yankees' David Cone pitched a perfect game in 1999, when he was a thirty-six-year-old entering the last stages of his career, or that Don Larsen and Yogi Berra, the battery of the most famous perfect game in history (Larsen's 1956 World Series masterpiece) were there to see it. Cone on the unlikelihood of his feat: "You probably have a better chance of winning the lottery than this happening, but what an honor," he said.

Comeback Kid

Few players in modern times have had the skill—or the bad luck—of Eric Davis. Possessed of an extraordinary blend of power and speed, Davis helped lead the Cincinnati Reds to the 1990 World Series—during which he lacerated his kidney diving for a fly ball. Further injuries led to his retirement after the 1994 season. But after a year away from the game, he returned to the Reds in 1996 (when this photo was taken), slamming 26 home runs, stealing 23 bases, and hitting .287.

Tribulation and Triumph

Eric Davis's superb—and star-crossed—career came to an end after this 2001 at-bat with the San Francisco Giants. Just four years earlier, he couldn't have even known that he'd be alive to enjoy the applause of fans and teammates. While playing with the Baltimore Orioles in 1997, Davis was diagnosed with colon cancer. He underwent surgery and chemotherapy...yet returned to play that same season, even hitting a home run in the Championship Series against the Indians.

Last of a Legend

By 1973, when this photo was taken, Willie Mays was at the end of his career. Playing for the Mets, he hit just .211. But he hadn't sacrificed the love and admiration people everywhere had for him, and no one was happier than his fans when he made it into one last postseason, even racking up a .286 batting average in the underdog Mets' seven-game loss to the Oakland A's. Soon after the Series ended, the great "Say-Hey Kid" said goodbye to baseball for good.

Yaz

No one bore the burden of the Curse of the Bambino more heavily than Carl Yastrzemski. As a twenty-eight-year-old in 1967, he hit for the Triple Crown and led the Miracle Sox to within a game of the World Series championship. Eight years later, he hit .455 in the playoffs and .310 in the World Series, only to see his Sox lose another classic seven-game Series, this time to Cincinnati. Then, in his last shot in 1978, he saw the Sox fall a game short of the Yankees in one of the most famous pennant races of all time. Too bad Yaz wasn't around to participate in the Sox' amazing 2004 Series run.

What Might Have Been

"An oasis of modesty in a desert of high-priced egos," in the words of *Sports Illustrated*'s Bruce Anderson, Don Mattingly (here "boning" his bat at the 1987 All-Star Game) seemed like a lock for the Hall of Fame his first four full years in the majors. (In 1985, for example, he hit .324 with 48 doubles, 35 home runs, and 145 RBI.) Then his back began to hurt, and his numbers dwindled, but he never lost his modesty and likeability, or the undying devotion of Yankee fans.

We Love You, Don

By 1995, his last season, injuries had worn Don Mattingly's glorious ability to mere competence. For a proud player who had enjoyed great success, ending with seasons of six and seven home runs must have been galling. The fans, however, understood what he was going through and honored him to the last. By retiring before the 1996 season, though, Mattingly missed by a single year being part of the next Yankee dynasty.

Another Comeback Kid

In 1994, just 34 years old and coming off a .300 season, Ryne Sandberg announced his retirement from the Chicago Cubs, saying, "I am not the type of person who can be satisfied with anything less than my very best effort and my very top performance." While the Cubs threw him this retirement party in 1995, they, and the Cubs' fans, were more than happy to see Ryno change his mind and return to the team in 1996. In his last two seasons, he added 37 home runs, 156 RBI, and more stellar glovework to his Hall of Fame record.

Where Does the Time Go?

Baseball fans of a certain age retain indelible images of Hall of Famers Bob Gibson, Lou Brock, and Warren Spahn, and of Joe Torre, a fine player in his own right and a lock Hall of Famer as manager of the New York Yankees. But this photograph doesn't necessarily reflect the image people hold on to: Seeing old timers is a bittersweet pleasure for fans, allowing them to glimpse their bygone heroes while also being reminded of the inevitable passage of the years.

Immortal

As steady and inexorable as a bulldozer, Hank Aaron chewed up the ground toward Babe Ruth's hallowed home run total of 714. Never hitting 50 homers in a season—but exceeding 40 fifteen times—Aaron added roughly 110 round-trippers to his total every three years... and he played for 23 seasons. His gradual but unstoppable approach left plenty of time for fans to appreciate his great skill and endurance, and to celebrate his accomplishments, even while his career was still under way.

The Manager

What does a star player do after his career comes to an end? Phil Niekro put off the answer to that question as long as he could, utilizing his stress-free knuckleball to stick around the majors until he was forty-eight years old. But the time eventually came, and Niekro made an interesting choice, deciding to manage the all-women Colorado Silver Bullets, who barnstormed the country playing men's teams. Here, Niekro consoles shortstop Toni Heisler after a tough inning.

Still Hustling

Mike Schmidt played hard from the day he arrived as a raw rookie in 1972. But by 1988, when this picture was taken, the writing was on the wall for the Phillies' magnificent third baseman. Seeing his skills erode was not acceptable for Schmidt, who hung up his spikes midseason in 1989, saying, "I could ask the Phillies to keep me on to add to my statistics, but my love for the game won't let me do that."

Looking Back

In his first full season, the Philadelphia Phillies' Mike Schmidt batted .196 in 367 at-bats, looking like the kind of raw slugger good pitchers could always get out. Instead, he soon developed into one of the most feared hitters of all time, with impressive power (548 HRs). On July 30, 1995 Schmidt was inducted into the Baseball Hall of Fame. Facing an enormous crowd of fans from the podium, he thanked them for "extending the Philadelphia city limits all the way to Cooperstown."

Old Friends

On September 27, 1996, two days before Ozzie Smith would play his final game, the St. Louis Cardinals held a celebration of his career. Among the attendees was Whitey Herzog, his manager during the glory years of the 1980s, when the charismatic Cardinals captured three pennants and a World Series. "Teams hated coming in here playing on those hot summer days," Smith recalled. "Willie McGee, Vince Coleman, Tommy [Herr], Whitey managing us—it was a great time."

The Road to Cooperstown

Faithful fans await the appearance of Ozzie Smith on his induction to the Hall of Fame, July 28, 2002. As many players do, Ozzie took the opportunity to speak of his greater ideals. "I sincerely believe that there is nothing truly great in any man or woman except their character, their willingness to move beyond the realm of self and into a greater realm of selflessness," said the Wizard in his induction speech. "Giving back is the ultimate talent in life."

It Ain't Over

As time goes on, some ballplayers seem to become emblems of the game. Yogi Berra is a perfect example. A three-time MVP with some of the greatest of Yankee teams, he marched directly into the Hall of Fame. But instead of fading slowly into history, Yogi went on to manage both the Mets and Yankees and then coach for decades. He even opened a baseball museum named after him in New Jersey. All this while uttering many of the greatest baseball sayings of all time!

The Pioneer

Always intelligent and opinionated, Hall of Famer Frank Robinson had long made it clear that he wanted to manage. In achieving his goal with the Cleveland Indians in 1975, he became the first African-American to helm a major-league team. Robinson never forgot who made it possible. "If I had one wish in the world today," he said upon becoming a manager, "it would be that Jackie Robinson could be here to see this happen."

Remembering Jackie

On April 15, 2007, the sixtieth anniversary of Jackie Robinson's debut with the Brooklyn Dodgers, Major League Baseball celebrated his breaking of the color line. Ceremonies were held across the country, and more than 200 ballplayers wore Robinson's Number 42 that day. "A life is not important except in the impact it has on other lives," Jackie once said, and by those standards, he lived one of the most important lives in baseball—and American—history.

An Honest Day's Work

By 1979, when this photo was taken, 40-year-old Gaylord Perry had been pitching for 17 years. He'd made more than 500 starts, and had won more than 275 games (of an eventual 314 victories). He was a middle-aged man in a young man's sport, but he had no desire to leave before he had to. The reason: An abiding love for the game. "The trouble with baseball," Perry once said, "is that it is not played the year round."

The Wanderer

Gaylord Perry was no journeyman—he was elected to the Hall of Fame in 1991—but at the end of a long career even a fine ballplayer can find himself having to check his uniform to remember what team he plays for. At the 1990 All-Star Game, Perry solved this problem in the simplest way possible.

The Father

His achievements may pale in comparison to his son Barry's, but Bobby Bonds was also one heck of a ballplayer. He slammed more than 30 home runs 6 times (when homers were much harder to come by than today), swiped as many as 48 bases in a season, and won three Gold Gloves. He also struck out abundantly (as many as 189 times in a season), but took the whiffs in stride, saying, "I don't see why you have to run down to first base every time to make an out."

One of 700+

Barry Bonds slugs a grand slam on his inevitable march to the home-run mark he set in 2007. Given the remarkable feats (and the controversy) that have marked Bonds' career, it's hard to remember that he once was measured against the achievements of his father, Bobby. "It's got to be tough playing under the shadow of his dad," said broadcaster Mike Shannon early in Barry's career. "But he doesn't let it bother him. He's got a lot of guts just to be out there."

Bonds and Bonds

Barry and Bobby never played together, but they did get the chance to wear the same uniform when Bobby joined the San Francisco Giants as a coach in 1993, the same year Barry signed with the team. It was Barry who got to wear the Giants' Number 25, just as his dad had during *his* stint with the team more than two decades earlier.

Like Father...

You wouldn't think, looking at this photo, that any child of Bob Boone's (he's the grimacing catcher being steamrolled by Rickey Henderson) would choose baseball as a profession. But you'd be wrong: Not just one, but two of his sons—Aaron and Bret—plunged ahead and became major leaguers as well. Of course, it was a longtime family tradition: Bob's dad, Ray, had been a talented infielder with the Cleveland Indians, Detroit Tigers, and other teams.

Like Son

Catchers (like Bob Boone) may be involved in more collisions than any other players, but they're not the only ones. Bob's son, Bret, chose to play second base, which left him in the sights of runners trying to break up the double play. Bret weathered the bumps and bruises to post a .266 batting average, 252 home runs, and 4 Gold Gloves during his 14-year career, which came to an end in 2005. Among them, the four Boones played for 56 seasons as of 2007.

Three Stars

San Diego coach—and former player—Sandy Alomar, Sr. (center), poses with his ballplaying sons, Sandy, Jr., (left), and Roberto, at the 1990 All-Star Game. Coming up, Sandy, Jr., felt that he and his brother had an advantage over other prospects. "You have the luxury of having a name," he said. After that, though, "It's up to you to make it. It doesn't matter that you're the son of a major-leaguer." Both he and Roberto earned their promotions, sticking around the bigs for nearly forty years combined.

Introducing the Griffeys

On August 30, 1990, the Ken Griffeys, Sr. and Jr., became the first father-and-son tandem ever to take the field as teammates. "I got to play with my dad. I got to go to work with him," Griffey raved to the *St. Louis Post-Dispatch* afterward. "That's the biggest thing that ever happened to me other than the days my kids were born." Just two weeks later, the two hit back-to-back home runs, a mark that seems unlikely ever to be repeated.

Brother Act

When Felipe, Jesus, and Matty Alou (shown here in 1973) took the field on September 15, 1963, for the San Francisco Giants, they became the first—and thus far, only—trio of brothers to man every outfield spot for the same team in a major-league game. Later, Jesus shrugged off the feat. "It was no big deal; we didn't telephone home or anything," he said. "After all, we played together all the time in winter ball in the Caribbean."

Never Let Go

Felipe Alou had an excellent career as a player, garnering more than 2,000 hits between 1958 and 1974. To a generation of younger fans, however, he's far better known as the smart, thoughtful manager of the Montreal Expos, whom he helmed between 1992 and 2001, and the San Francisco Giants (2003–06). "I wish I could just sit on a rocking chair," he said in 2005, when he turned seventy. "Just bring me a rocking chair in the dugout." But he didn't really mean it—the lure of baseball was just too strong.

Prodigal Son

With a father (Felipe), two uncles (Matty and Jesus), and two cousins (Mel Rojas and Jose Sosa) with major-league experience, it's no surprise that Moises Alou was destined for the Show as well. Still, no one could have guessed he'd end up as one of the best of the entire clan, hitting as high as .355, driving in as many as 124 runs, accumulating more than 2,000 career hits, and exceeding 30 home runs three times.

The Next Generation?

Well, maybe not. But as long ago as 1901, when the American League was formed as a cleaner, less rowdy—and therefore more fan friendly—alternative to the older N.L., baseball officials and players have understood the need to appeal to a younger audience, and girls in particular. What Colorado catcher Joe Girardi is doing here is providing a lifetime's glowing memory for this little fan.

Future Stars

Ken Griffey, Sr., sits flanked by grandson Trey (left) and Shane Larkin, the son of Cincinnati Reds shortstop Barry, in 1999. Predicted Peter Gammons in 2005, when Trey was eleven: "If he doesn't go to college to be a premier running back, he will be the first pick in the 2012 draft." And with his heritage—Barry was a 12-time All-Star who retired with 2,340 hits and a .295 batting average—Shane might have just as promising a future.

The Appreciation Was Mutual

Nothing beats getting dirty on a major-league diamond, as these boys discovered at the 1994 Fan Appreciation Day in Busch Stadium, St. Louis. Sometimes the distance between the stands and the field can seem miles wide, but days like this help shrink it—and strengthen fans' loyalty at the same time.

Joy at Any Age

Whether it's this Toms River, New Jersey, team celebrating a game won in the 1998 Little League Series, a big-league player crossing the plate, or a bunch of kids in a Saturday pickup game in the park, the expressions on the faces are the same. The game of baseball is a great leveler—you don't have to be the biggest, the fastest, or the strongest kid to make a great catch or score the winning run. The dream of baseball is everybody's dream.

The Moment

So much of baseball revolves around waiting. In this age of speed and noise and instant gratification, the slow pace drives some people crazy. But for the millions of true fans, the quiet before the big moment is part of baseball's appeal, because it makes the moment—the game-winning home run, the highlight-reel catch, the strikeout or stolen base—even more thrilling when it finally comes.